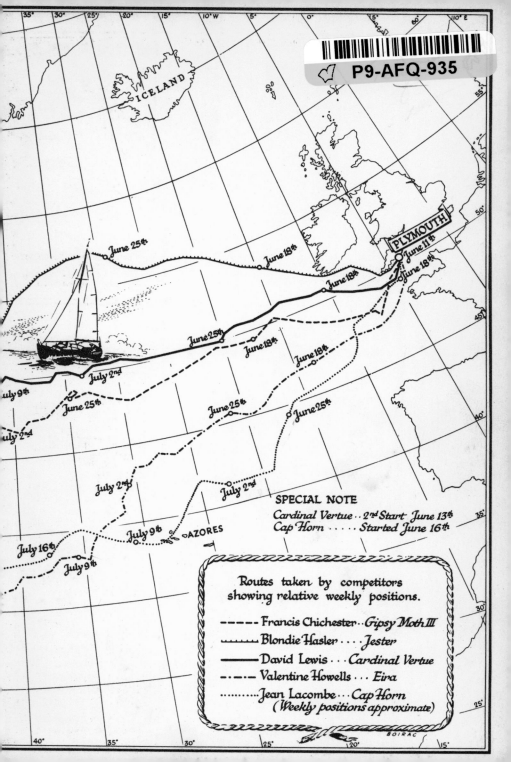

ICELAND

PLYMOUTH

June 25th June 18th June 18th June 11th June 18th

June 25th June 18th June 18th

July 2nd June 25th June 25th June 25th

July 9th June 25th

July 2nd

July 2nd July 2nd

July 9th AZORES

July 16th July 9th

July 9th

SPECIAL NOTE
Cardinal Vertue .. 2nd Start June 13th
Cap Horn ..... Started June 16th

Routes taken by competitors
showing relative weekly positions.

----- Francis Chichester..*Gipsy Moth III*
.... Blondie Hasler .... *Jester*
——— David Lewis ... *Cardinal Vertue*
–·–·– Valentine Howells ... *Eira*
.... Jean Lacombe.... *Cap Horn*
(*Weekly positions approximate*)

BOIRAC

THE SHIP WOULD NOT TRAVEL DUE WEST

"But the principal failing occurred in the sailing,
And the Bellman, perplexed and distressed,
Said he *had* hoped, at least, when the wind blew due East,
That the ship would *not* travel due West!"

—LEWIS CARROLL

THE SHIP
WOULD NOT TRAVEL
DUE WEST

by

DAVID LEWIS

ST MARTIN'S PRESS

NEW YORK

ACKNOWLEDGMENTS

I CANNOT thank individually all those people, family, friends, colleagues and strangers, who gave me moral support, hospitality, wrote encouraging letters, lent me gear or worked patiently preparing *Cardinal Vertue*. They are too numerous for me to make mention of them all, but theirs was the Atlantic crossing. Their kindness was a tangible force always present aboard, which did not allow me to let them down too badly.

But these I must mention in public acknowledgment of my indebtedness:

The Flag Officers and members of the Royal Western Yacht Club, the Slocum Society, the Royal Burnham Yacht Club, the Little Ship Club, the Sheepshead Bay Yacht Club and the New York Yacht Club.

Lieutenant-Colonel H. G. Hasler and Valentine Howells for their accurate and patient work in completing the medical logs which needed up to an hour a day, and for permission to quote from their published and unpublished accounts.

Commander W. B. Luard, R.N. Retd. for his patient advice and for reading the manuscript of this book at many stages, correcting innumerable errors in spelling and punctuation, and pointing out nautical solecisms and lapses from good taste, and Mr. A. J. Law for helping to remove some of the clichés.

Doctors L. E. Wall, J. J. and L. G. E. De Jode, and Dr. D. J. Gorham, the colleagues who alone made my holiday possible.

The following companies generously donated their products and helped me in many ways: Thomas Walker and Son Ltd., British Nylon Spinners Ltd., Marine Electronics, Stanley Tools Ltd., Pfizer Ltd., John Wyeth and Bros. Ltd., B.C.B. Ltd., Horlicks Ltd., Smith and Nephew Ltd., Scientific Pharmaceutics, Lea Bridge Industries Ltd., Imperial Chemical Industries Ltd., Expanded Rubber Co. Ltd., Jablo Plastics Industries Ltd., Eastwood Plastics Ltd., Minnesota Mining and Manufacturing Co. Ltd.

I have made specific acknowledgment in Appendix Four, "Research Observations", and in Appendix Five, "Treatment of Sea-serpent Stings and Other Ailments", for much valued help and advice in their compilation.

Acknowledgment is also gladly made to authors, their executors and publishers, and the Controller of H.M. Stationery Office, for quotations in text and appendices as follows:

James A. Mitchener: *Return to Paradise* (Random House Inc., New York); D. P. Capper: *The Vikings of Britain* (George Allen and Unwin Ltd., London); "The Orkneyingers' Saga" in *The Icelandic Sagas*, vol. 3, 1894 (H.M.S.O., London); Francis Chichester: *Alone Across the Atlantic* (George

Allen and Unwin Ltd., London) and articles in *The Observer*, July 24, 31 and Aug. 7, 1960; Edward Reman: *The Norse Discoveries and Explorations in America* (University of California Press, Berkeley and Los Angeles); Gaythorne Hardy: *The Norse Discoveries of America* (The Clarendon Press, Oxford); Rudyard Kipling's verses from "Harp Song of the Dane Women" in *Puck of Pook's Hill* (Mrs. G. Bambridge and Macmillan and Co. Ltd., London); Extracts from an article by the author in the *Journal of the College of General Practitioners*, Feb., 1960; *Nova Scotia and Bay of Fundy Pilot*, 1958 (The Admiralty and H.M.S.O., London); *Nantucket Sound: Esso Cruising Guide* (Esso Standard Oil Co., U.S.A.); James Fisher: *Bird Recognition, 1* (Penguin Books Ltd., Harmondsworth); Humphrey Barton: *Atlantic Adventures* (Adlard Coles Ltd., Southampton); George Barker: verses from "Galway Bay" in *The Faber Book of Modern Verse* (Faber and Faber Ltd., London); Louis MacNeice: verses from "Bagpipe Music" in *The Earth Compels* (Faber and Faber Ltd., London); Wilfred Noyce: verses from *Springs of Adventure* (John Murray Ltd., London); *North Sea Pilot*, vol. I, 1910, and *Newfoundland and Labrador Pilot*, 8th edn., 1951 (The Admiralty and H.M.S.O., London).

For figures reproduced on p. 134, of *Vertue* with masthead sloop rig: Douglas Phillips-Birt's article "The Vertues" in *The Yachtsman*, Aug., 1960; on p. 136, of *Vertue* plan: Humphrey Barton's *Vertue XXXV* (Rupert Hart-Davis, The Mariners Library, no. 31); on p. 143, of *Gipsy Moth III:* Francis Chichester's *Alone Across the Atlantic* (George Allen and Unwin, London); and also on p. 143, of *Cap Horn:* M. J. J. Herbulot and Soc. Cidevyv, Paris.

Finally, I would single out one among the many unnamed friends to represent the rest: the elderly lady who gave me a cloth and wire wishbone which assuredly brought me luck.

FOREWORD

by H. G. HASLER

THE first public announcement of the impending Single-handed Transatlantic Race was made in August 1957, nearly three years before the race was due to start. In the next eighteen months, a great number of inquiries, requests, and criticisms were received from dozens of prospective entrants, not one of whom subsequently came anywhere near the starting-line.

There was, then, nothing out of the ordinary in the letter that reached me on March 30, 1959, from a Dr. D. H. Lewis, asking for further details of the race on behalf of "some friends" who were "interested", even though it did not need second sight to guess who the "friends" were. I sent him a routine reply, and thought no more of it until six months later, when a second letter revealed that he had spent part of the intervening time in "wandering off to Norway in *Cardinal Vertue*", and that his single-handed passages from Burnham-on-Crouch to Stavanger and back had already been accepted by the Slocum Society as qualifying him to enter the race.

This made me sit up. For the first time, it seemed as if we had a serious entrant on our hands. Ten days later, when he came to see me at Curdridge, I realized that this was an understatement: what we had on our hands was somebody who was going to sail that damned race if it killed him. From this time on, I knew that the race was really going to happen.

David Lewis is not a large man physically, but he has the hard muscular development of an athlete. Mentally, as any reader of this book will discover, he is modest, generous, humorous, dedicated, and painfully honest. There are no heroics here, but many confessions of clumsiness, of stupidity, and of ordinary wholesome fear, that will at once ring true to anybody who has ever taken a small sailing boat across open water. I only doubt whether most of us would have had the moral courage to record them so accurately.

At Plymouth, in the last nightmare days before the start, when David and I seemed to be holding a private competition in unreadiness, he still found time to turn over, as a gift to each competitor, a splendid outfit of medical and emergency stores that he had been assembling

vii

for months past. It was typical of him to spend precious time doing this, instead of checking through his own provisions and ship's stores, which later proved, in mid-Atlantic, to be incomplete.

By the time the starting-gun fired, David had already faced and overcome a great number of serious difficulties. Three and a half hours later, I made out—far ahead of me—*Cardinal Vertue* with only the stump of her mast left standing. Surely even David couldn't do much to redeem *that* situation?

This book shows how very wrong I was. *Cardinal Vertue* may well be the only racing yacht that has ever appeared on the prize list after having been dismasted three thousand miles short of the finishing line. After the race, his single-handed passage back from Newfoundland to the Shetlands was remarkable for a succession of heavy gales, and for the way in which the boat and the man stood up to them.

I admire David Lewis both for what he did, and for the way he tells it.

Curdridge, Hampshire.
September 1961.

CONTENTS

CONTENTS

APPENDICES

PLATES

*

[The author's drawings in the text are from the Log of *Cardinal Vertue*.]

I

FIVE SAILS TO THE WESTWARD

"When the winds blow my mast will go."
East Coast Bargeman's Song.

THIS is not a yachtsman's log-book, nor is it merely the story of a race. It will try to tell something of men's feelings, of their fears and of their laughter as through victory and defeat they test their skill, judgment and endurance against the impersonal Atlantic.

By its nature this account must be an intensely personal one, for only my own experience can be described at first hand. However, the daily records of emotions, sleep, food, and events at sea, which were kept by some of the competitors in the Single-handed Transatlantic Sailing Race to further medical research, have been drawn upon with their authors' permission.

The competitive aspect of the race was outweighed, for me at all events, by the struggle between man and natural forces. The adventure itself assumed greater depth and purpose from the clearer understanding we hoped to gain of man's reactions when he stands revealed, stripped of all outside support, in a struggle, and alone with his soul.

So the problem of scientific investigation into the mental and physical experiences underlying the fight to inch westward towards the Americas, provided its own exciting challenge to the intellect; though for me, the ultimate test was to come after the race itself was over, when I kept a rendezvous, in remote high latitudes, with the storm winds of autumn.

A week before the race four of us were at Plymouth working feverishly on our boats, making last-minute preparations: Francis Chichester with his 39-foot yawl *Gipsy Moth III*; "Blondie" Hasler, who had called his 25-foot modified Folkboat, *Jester*, because she was "such a bloody joke"; Valentine Howells with his 25-foot Folkboat *Eira* and myself with *Cardinal Vertue*, a 25-foot Vertue-class sloop.

Jean Lacombe, caught by heavy weather in the Channel while sailing across from France in the little 21-foot French sloop *Cap Horn*, arrived at Plymouth only on the eve of the race. He crossed the starting-line five days after the other boats.

Arthur Piver, an American, with a most unusual craft, a 30-foot trimaran, sailed over from the United States with two companions, but reached Plymouth too late to compete.

I had been doing a *locum* for the friend who was to look after my patients during most of my absence, so there had been little time to prepare the innumerable things necessary for a three thousand miles voyage. The final week proved hectic; radio transmitters, which had been lent to us, were being installed by the Navy; I had to sort out and pack medical kits and "survival" food packs for each competitor; emergency gear—flares, inflatable rafts and other items had to be collected. These were being supplied by the manufacturers largely through Mr. E. C. B. Lee, Secretary to the Naval Life Saving Committee, who wrote dozens of "baited" letters somewhat as follows:

". . . If there are any items of equipment which you would like evaluated . . . you could get in touch direct with Dr. David H. Lewis, who is co-ordinating the activities. These adventurous sailors also intend to make the return voyage single-handed. The weather is then liable to be stormy so it is *possible that a survival incident may occur.*" (My italics.)

A friend and I, under the auspices of the Medical Research Council, had prepared "medical log-books" in which to keep daily records of food, drink, sleep and emotions. Those who agreed to collaborate in this study had to be weighed and their food listed, a procedure to be repeated immediately upon arrival in New York. John Harries, of the Food Science Division of the Ministry of Agriculture and Fisheries, came to Plymouth to assist me in this work but even with his help there was so much to be done that I never did find time to make a list of food I should need myself.

Into the existing chaos there suddenly descended upon us hordes of reporters from the Press, TV and radio. Each morning, soon after we began work on our yachts, we were besieged, and from then on were interviewed almost continuously throughout the day. Although we became hardened to being constantly photographed, it was not until late evening that we were able to continue undisturbed.

I had not fully appreciated the possibility of non-slip decks until I found that Howells' and Hasler's were like sandpaper; you could not slip if you tried. This had been achieved by sprinkling silver sand over an ordinary undercoat while it was still wet and, after it had dried, brushing off the surplus sand and overpainting with a top coat. We scoured Plymouth day in and day out to find some silver sand.

Eventually Cicely, one of my most hard-worked friends, discovered some, not in a paint shop, but in the market, where it was being sold as roughage for canaries! After the reporters had gone she and my son, Barry, spent the evenings, whenever it was not raining, painting and sanding the decks of *Cardinal Vertue*.

There was much discussion among us about which route we would take. The northern one is shorter but runs through the iceberg zone and the winds are contrary. The southern route with the steady favourable trade winds and the Gulf Stream is much longer. We were all very frank about our plans except Francis Chichester, and Francis was being very cagey. We did not know which way he was going until one day he went shopping with Val Howells and bought a great length of fishing net which he said was to drape round the stanchions of his ship in order to catch any flying fish that skimmed aboard. Flying fish frequent the warm southern waters, so this finally convinced us that he was going to take the northern route!

The reporters, photographers and radio and television people who kept coming to see us were very long suffering. One, who was asking me questions, seemed so interested that I became carried away. Holding forth about the tactics of the race, I forgot he was not a sailor. I was trying to explain how a growth of weed on a ship's hull would slow her down and how this would occur more quickly in warm waters than in cold.

"So not only is the northern route the shortest, and not only do you have a favourable current for the last twelve hundred miles, but what becomes most important of all after a month at sea, is the state of the bottom. You see the cold water of the Labrador current is good for it."

He looked startled, and then with a great effort rallied manfully: "Oh yes—ah—hygiene—so important of course."

Every day now I would climb 34 feet to the top of the mast to become accustomed to the effort and balance involved in doing so, just in case this proved necessary at sea. At first it was difficult. I would cling on so tightly out of sheer fright that I would have no energy left for climbing; but after a time the rhythm of my movements became more automatic until I could scramble quickly up, right to the mast-head, without very much trouble.

3

The day before we were due to start Jean Lacombe arrived from France. His little plywood *Cap Horn* had bounced up and down in a Channel gale until Jean, who is short, stocky and very, very tough, sailed in exhausted. That night as we sat in a restaurant somebody rushed over towards me.

"The Frenchman has fainted, come quickly."

Jean had not fainted, he was lying with his head on the table, not unconscious but simply fast asleep. He could not get his boat ready in time to set off with the rest of us, so he planned to leave about five days later.

Meanwhile, we heard that Piver's trimaran *Nimble* had reached the Azores from America in three weeks. This was good going, the only snag being that the Azores lie about twelve hundred miles south of England, so it was doubtful whether he could reach Plymouth within the two weeks from the official start allowed by the rules for latecomers. Why did he head so far south? This remained a source of endless speculation, not answered until we met some of the trimaran's crew later in New York. Calms and fogs had delayed their progress for a few days. Then after clearing Nantucket the first north-west gale had struck. Gales and strong winds from the north and north-west had continued for ten days. They were forced to run before or partly across the seas and though *Nimble* surfed across the face of the combers at 15 knots they were carried several hundred miles south of their course. The Azores lay eight hundred miles ahead; America over a thousand miles astern. They made the best of the situation and made their landfall at the Azores. After provisioning, they continued to Plymouth, running before favourable winds. They returned by air after leaving their craft at Plymouth.

A welcome visitor during our preparations was John Pflieger, Commodore of the Slocum Society, but there was hardly time to speak to him in all the bustle. I am afraid I tried my friends sorely. One, a German student, hitch-hiked down from London twice to help with the preparations, yet I do not think I ever found the time to thank him. Another practically made me a radio set. An echo-sounder had been lent to me. Michael Chandler had spent his whole holiday working aboard. There was a sextant borrowed from Tom Moncrief, who teaches navigation at Lerwick in the Shetland Islands. My own yacht club, the Royal Burnham, had noticed my habit of running aground on every convenient sandbank and had sent me some charts. As I had removed the propeller before leaving Burnham to allow the use

4

of the engine for charging the battery during the race, *Cardinal Vertue*, relying on sails alone, had been "on the putty" more often than usual.

Humphrey Barton came and looked over my rigging for me. In 1950 he, and Kevin O'Riordan, sailed *Vertue XXXV* (*Cardinal Vertue* is Vertue XIX) from Falmouth to New York in forty-seven days, encountering a hurricane in which the gallant little ship, lying to a sea anchor streamed from her starboard sheet-winch, was picked up bodily by a sea and thrown down on her port cabin top. The wood split, the glass disintegrated and water poured in. The two men are the only ones I know of who owe their lives to dyspepsia. For Humphrey Barton is highly-strung and thin; thin enough to wriggle through the shattered window to reach the pump in the cockpit. Their voyage was historic in that it showed how a small, modern yacht could sail across the Atlantic in face of the prevailing westerlies. If this was possible on the intermediate route passing near the Azores, which Barton and O'Riordan had taken, then the shorter northern route must be practicable, too.

Barry, my eleven-year-old son, was everywhere. He was fascinated above all by Hasler's boat, with its ingenious Chinese junk rig. As soon as we reached Plymouth he was aboard, full of questions and more questions. I thought:

"Here at last I have my secret weapon against Hasler."

But I had underestimated him. Before five minutes had passed there was an understanding between them. Barry had been rationed to fifty questions to start with, plus five every subsequent hour. "Blondie" kindly but firmly kept him to this agreement.

Barry was incensed to see a newspaper report in which his father was described as a bachelor.

"And what about me?" he asked indignantly.

I tried to explain.

"Well I was married, but I'm married no longer, so that really does count as a bachelor, doesn't it."

He still looked rather doubtful.

"Anyway, don't keep calling me 'Venerable Ancestor'," I snapped peevishly.

Barry was really brooding over the unfair single-handed rule that had stopped him accompanying me.

"But we sailed to Holland together last autumn and we'll sail up to the Norwegian fjords next summer," I said, trying to comfort him.

"Anyway you often complain that I am bad tempered and swear at you at sea."

"The Norwegian Sea isn't the same as the Atlantic," said Barry, still not mollified.

I had expected a friend to drive my daughter, Anna, down, but she had not arrived and one evening after I had turned in tired out by interviews, a man's voice hailed from the quayside.

"Is Doctor Lewis aboard there?"

I sleepily opened the hatch and peered up at two dim figures. Then with considerable presence of mind attained by years of medical practice, I replied:

"I'm sorry but you've just missed him, he sank half an hour ago."

I stepped down and firmly closed the hatch; then was stopped by a patient if somewhat exasperated feminine voice.

"Daddy, it's me."

The night before the start racing flags were broken out from our starboard cross-trees to flap and crackle in a gusty south-west wind. From Howells' *Eira* flew the Red Dragon, the standard of Wales. Francis Chichester sported a Gipsy Moth. Hasler's *Jester* remained uncompromisingly bare. *Cardinal Vertue's* standard, embroidered by Cicely with a kiwi and its large egg, went aloft on a rope and wire halyard. Tomorrow the flags would be at mastheads in place of our club burgees, remaining aloft until we reached New York—or gave up.

Hasler and I were working on board our boats until nearly three that morning. At seven we were picked up by the launches which towed us outside the dock into a small naval harbour, where we attempted to scrub the oil and grease off the hulls.

For weeks we had had fine easterlies, but now it was blowing hard, overcast, dismal westerly weather, with rain squalls scudding across the bay. The forecast was for a south-west headwind of force 7, nearly gale strength. I felt forlorn and miserable. How could the others be so calm? Later, I learnt that each had had the same feeling.

Anna turned up again in time to be press-ganged into cooking me some breakfast. We all felt very tense as I brusquely said goodbye to the children.

Then we were towed outside the little harbour. As we hoisted sail, suddenly everything was transformed. Sailing close past me, Val Howells called out:

"It's all right now, David, isn't it?"

"Yes," I replied, and I meant it.

6

We were cruising up and down behind the starting-line, sizing up the course down the Sound, watching the signal flags and waiting for the starting-gun, hardly aware of the launches and yachts that rolled and pitched on every side. I saw a burst of flashes from an Aldis lamp at the naval dockyard. It seemed to go on and on, then was answered briefly by a naval launch that swung round, put on speed and pounded towards us. Her decks were crowded with guests. I noticed the Royal Western Yacht Club Commodore and his wife, and Chris Brasher from *The Observer* wearing a grin from ear to ear. As they came near an amused naval officer called through a loud hailer.

"A telegram for you just been flashed across to us—

'*K. M. sends you her love*'."

There were ribald cheers from the launch. I grinned spontaneously. Of all the women I had known in my pleasant "bachelor" life "K. M." was the most poised, the most cautious and the most discreet. It must have cost her great heart-searching before she had sent me a message at all, and here was her indiscretion being broadcast across Plymouth Sound!

Perhaps I remember this incident because my sense of humour was soon to become the first casualty of the race.

Now we began jockeying for position. The five-minute gun sounded and, sheeting our sails hard in, we lay over to the fresh breeze, racing for the line as a puff of smoke from the starting gun drifted over the water, and the starting flag fluttered down from the flagstaff below Plymouth Hoe. Hasler shot away, his hull clearing the starboard-hand buoy by no more than a few inches. After him came the rest of us, out into the Sound, hard on the wind. A quick tack to clear the breakwater, then our ships were plunging as they met the swell of the open sea. Three thousand miles to go now and the land soon began to drop astern.

We had started at ten o'clock in the morning. At eleven-thirty, during a lull, I hoisted the big headsail, the genoa, and now *Cardinal Vertue*, heeling over with water streaming over the lee deck, threshed seawards. The others had gained on me while I was shifting sails, with Chichester well ahead; but soon I passed Hasler and was rapidly overhauling Howells.

We left the Eddystone Lighthouse, set on its jagged shark-tooth rocks, to starboard. Pressed down by the increasing wind *Cardinal Vertue* was going fast, but, over-canvased, she pounded so hard into the steep head seas that everything down below, even the heavy spare

Calor gas cylinders which had been well lashed down, shook and jumped. Yet she was sailing really well, and Howells' *Eira* was not far ahead. Hasler lay astern but to windward.

At 1.30 p.m., without warning, my mast snapped cleanly 12 feet above the deck, and the upper 22 feet crashed over the port quarter into the sea beside me. I clutched the tiller for several seconds unable to believe that this wallowing hulk, strewn with tangled wreckage, was my beautiful ship which seconds before had danced proudly with the ocean's winds and had seemed so alive. If only she would sink quickly taking me with her!

Then, still shocked, I was acting automatically. The mast had to be brought up on deck before it pounded a hole in the ship's side and tore the sails to pieces. Sobbing with exertion, and with hands cut and bleeding, I tore away the lightning conductor which was attached to the mast by small sharp tacks, until I could slide the broken end far enough along the deck to reach its top and unshackle the mainsail. Next, I slid the upper half of the sail down its track on to the deck and hauled the mast right aboard, until it projected across the pulpit forward, and over the port quarter astern. Then I lashed it down and pulled the sail and the festoons of rigging aboard.

While I was doing this, wading thigh deep in tangled wires and ropes, I was wondering whether the rest of the mast was about to go, in which case I would be carried down, inextricably tangled in a web of rigging, into the tossing sea on which my dismasted wreck was rolling so wildly.

Now I had time to look at the damage. The sail seemed all right, the mast also intact and well stayed up to the broken cross-trees. It had broken cleanly. There must have been a fault somewhere, but exactly where remained to be seen later.

It was clear that there was only one possible thing to be done. This was to set up some sort of jury rig with which to sail back to Plymouth, then to have the mast repaired as quickly as possible so that I could carry on with the race.

I rummaged below for No. 3 staysail, climbed up the wildly gyrating mast to the cross-trees, and clinging on with great difficulty, slipped a block over them and threaded a halyard through it. With this small staysail hoisted the ship had steerage way. So at 1.50 p.m. I was able to turn her nose towards the distant smudge of land.

Hasler now came up with me. He had been sailing slower but further to windward than the rest of us. He circled round, his unconventional rig giving him perfect control in trimming his sheets instantly and in reducing his sail area at will.

"David, can I go and get help?" he cried. "If I sail to the Eddystone they will send for a tow."

"I don't want a tow," I replied. "It's all O.K. I'm sailing back to Plymouth to get this damned mast fixed, then I will see you in New York."

Blondie seemed very doubtful and most reluctant to leave me.

"It *is* all right," I called again. "Look, she is under control already, I'm heading back."

So with a final wave Blondie set out on course again and *Jester* rapidly faded into the grey murk to windward.

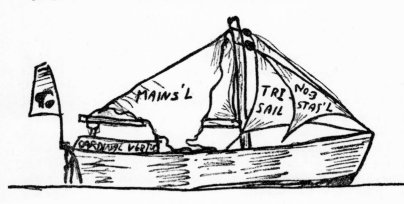

Only twenty minutes had passed between the mast going over the side and the ship again being under way and heading for Plymouth. I climbed the mast once more and rigged another block on which I hoisted the trisail to act as a second headsail. With these two headsails and the lower half of the mainsail, she began to close the dim Devon hills fourteen miles away, moving at about two knots and steering with the wind vane self-steering gear. There was time to drink several mugs of water and eat a bar of fudge and to write in the log:

"Now for Plymouth, a quick repair and on with the race."

I lashed my racing flag with its broken shaft to the starboard rigging as a sign that *Cardinal Vertue* was still racing. It was heartening to see the gallant kiwi aloft again. By 3 p.m. I was abreast of the Eddystone and making good progress. Nevertheless, it was hard to return.

This adventure had started the wrong way round. There had been publicity and praise for what we were *going to* do before we had done anything at all. During the past week we had been speaking on radio and television and giving interviews to newspapers. We had been admired as the clever people who were about to sail the Atlantic; now here was I, after a tremendous send off, returning the same day in a supreme anti-climax. I did not feel at all good about it and swore that I would move the very heavens to have that mast mended quickly.

For the moment there was nothing to be done but to make coffee. *Cardinal Vertue* continued to steer herself in towards the land that still lay shrouded in squalls and low cloud. Two and a half knots now! Some yachts racing nearby passed close, but none seemed to notice anything unusual.

This annoyed me; surely they did not think people went sailing on purpose with such stumpy masts as I had now? It seemed an age until at 7.35 p.m. I passed the outer breakwater and entered Plymouth harbour.

Now I urgently needed a tow to bring me right in. Off Drake's Island a pilot boat threw me a line and brought me into Millbay Docks. I saw we were about to bring up alongside a yacht that was moored there. Suddenly I saw its name, *Cohoe III*.

"Oh no!" I thought, "anywhere but here!"

For Adlard Coles the owner, had sailed his first *Cohoe* from Bermuda to the U.S.A., weathering the hurricane in which *Vertue XXXV* was almost lost, and had then raced back to Bermuda and gone on to win the Bermuda to England race of 1950. His book *North Atlantic* is a classic. Rather than meet a man like this, I felt I would sooner crawl into a quiet hole somewhere to hide. But Adlard and his wife helped me make fast, looked after me, fed me, and protected me from too many interruptions.

As soon as I had touched land I had made frantic telephone calls desperately seeking someone to mend the mast that very night. So one later interruption was very welcome. Mr. Mashford, head of a famous yard at Cremyll, across the River Tamar, came aboard in a flapping raincoat, carefully looked over the damage, and then said in his deliberate, West Country way:

"You will be able to leave by, say, Monday midday."

It was then Saturday night, and to be able to sail on Monday was far better than I had dared to hope for. Yet somehow, this seemingly casual statement inspired more confidence than a thousand flowery promises. Life became worth living again.

"I'll pick her up with a towing launch at six o'clock in the morning," he said, and then departed.

Now that I could relax, I realized just how desperately tired I was. But before I climbed sleepily back to my own ship Adlard Coles said something which further lightened my gloom.

"If you ever want to write a book about this race," he said, "come to me for a bit of advice about it and perhaps some help in publishing it."

How could anybody still have such confidence in me after what had happened? Those encouraging words supported me greatly in the days that lay ahead.

I did not wake next morning when Mashford's launch took *Cardinal Vertue* in tow. I was still asleep as we crossed the Tamar, which forms the Devon-Cornwall border, and docked on the other side at Cremyll. When I sleepily came on deck, still early on this Sunday morning, I found that half the employees, and most of the Mashford family, too, had turned out, quietly and purposefully, as if it were the most natural thing in the world and nothing special at all. Within a quarter of an hour the mast was out of *Cardinal Vertue*, the sails were ashore to be checked over and dried ready for repair. The rigging and fittings were being stripped off the mast and the work was well under way.

Soon telegrams of commiseration, greetings and good cheer came flooding in. Friends like Bill Luard, Ritchie Seymour, and people from the Royal Western Yacht Club came over from Plymouth to help.

My daughter, Anna, arrived. It was a delight and comfort to have her there. Barry had already left for London, driving with friends. They opened the Sunday paper that morning.

"My God, David has had an accident!" Barry had turned dead white and snatched the paper, but after a few moments he handed it back, and regaining the unconcern proper to a schoolboy of eleven, remarked casually:

"Oh, it's only his mast, he broke one last year, he is always breaking them."

George Armitage, owner of *Temptress*, the famous ship in which Edward Allcard made several Atlantic passages, took me off to breakfast aboard this wonderful old yawl. I felt much better afterwards and set to work to make the ship ready for sea again.

Meanwhile, word came that Hasler had been sighted closing the Lizard, and had rounded it, in the teeth of a contrary wind of force 7 and, he told me later, in spite of seasickness. There had been no news of the others, but I learnt later that Chichester was by then really tearing along well out towards the western approaches of the Channel. His last sight of the others had been of Howells passing him while he was rolling down a reef, so for the rest of the voyage he was haunted by visions of the "bearded Viking".

But Howells soon met trouble. His 100-lb. battery was lashed firmly in the forecastle. Water, trickling through the forehatch as *Eira* pounded into head seas, had caused the lashings to shrink, so that they had torn away the whole side of the battery. Corrosive acid came pouring out over his fresh vegetables, over clothes, over everything. The battery had to be thrown overboard, leaving Val without lights as the darkness descended on his first stormy night at sea.

Jean Lacombe, unhurried as ever, came to see me. In 1956 he had crossed the Atlantic alone in the 18-foot *Hippocampe* from Toulon to Puerto Rico, and thence to New York. Although the yacht which he was sailing this time was 21 feet long, it was much lighter; so light that it would dance to every ripple, and it was very small. Yet how calm he was compared with me, who was all a flurry of nerves and impatience! He expressed surprise that I was hoping to be away as soon as Monday.

"Me, I will leave Thursday," he said, phlegmatic as ever, unaffected by the excitement and tenseness of it all. And leave on Thursday he did, to face in some ways the greatest ordeal.

2

TO THE WEST—OVER SEA

THIS one day at Cremyll, under the shadow of Mount Edgcumbe, busy as it was, gave me breathing space to become aware of that green rolling Devon-Cornwall border country, to which I was saying good-bye.

A few days earlier, Lord Morley, Vice-Commodore of the Royal Western Yacht Club, had entertained us in his lovely home at Saltram. He had toasted us.

"Four gallant gentlemen of England, adventuring forth westward in your little ships in the spirit of those who set out from the West Country in other times."

Perhaps his words in such a setting had conjured up an evocation of an imaginary Elizabethan England, of some idealized never-never land. Nevertheless, I felt that I was saying goodbye to something of England which was real and part of me, as I had been born here, across the river in Plymouth.

However, my earliest memories are of New Zealand, where I was taken as a baby. It was my mother's country and to it I owe the shaping of my childhood and young manhood. By a strange twist in the skein of kinship, my very first sea adventure had been with my cousin Val Edgcumbe, younger brother to the heir of the Mount Edgcumbe estate, which backed the little port where I now lay.

I can still vividly recall sitting on the bottom boards of a dinghy in the hot sunshine, watching with awe while an almost grown up Val set sail and steered us confidently out to sea. Stark-etched, too, in memory is the look on my father's face after he had rescued us. Years later I mentioned the incident to my mother.

"I suppose Val was about eighteen?" I asked.

She looked at me quizzically.

"Well not quite, you were five and he was eleven."

With some amusement I now remembered a letter from Val written from New Zealand when he heard that I was entering the Transatlantic Race. After a few remarks about the family he continued, obviously following a train of thought inspired by the enterprise on which I was to embark.

"Three New Zealanders were wrecked off Australia last week and lost their craft, and a few months back quite a big yacht, which had set off on a world cruise was caught in a gale off North Cape. Dismasted, she was subsequently rolled over twice in heavy seas, but survived and was taken in tow by a Japanese ship and brought into Auckland. I have had some good fishing lately. . . . I can see by the news that you are having terrible gales in Europe and many ships have been lost with all hands, including a lifeboat on the English coast. The *Holm Glen* was lost with all hands off Timeru last month. No one knows the cause of the disaster. She was 15 per cent. above strength for A1 classification at Lloyds. A new ship and the weather was not particularly bad. Would you please write from New York and let us know how the Race went. We should be most interested to hear of your experiences."

I thought wryly that if my experiences were those he obviously expected, the chances of my arriving in New York at all were remote!

Here in this gentle corner of England I looked back on yet another farewell; a farewell to my father's land, and to the rugged Welsh mountains among which he had spent many happy hours.

During the winter I had twice sought the high hills. Once it was to clamber along airy Grib Goch, the Red Ridge of Snowdon which was thickly covered in new snow at the time and almost Alpine in character. I had been unsteady, unused to the height, for I had not climbed for a long time; but I had decided that my will-power needed toning up. Life in a big city provides little opportunity to test the nervous system's ability to drive us forward against physical fear. It seemed to me that practice in self-control was needed, and would pay dividends in the months to come.

On the second occasion we crossed over Tryfan and Glyder Fawr. When we were descending the Devil's Kitchen—of which my father had often spoken—a great gash in the mountain-side now packed with snow—I untied from the rope, left the others, and kicked steps up into a black cleft laced with monstrous fluted icicles. There I stood alone for a little while looking down the Nantffrancon valley past Bangor, where my father had lived, to the silver gleam of the Menai Straits and the smudge of the Isle of Anglesey beyond. I felt in communion with my father and seemed to be imbued with something of the spirit of this ancient land, and to be granted strength from those wild crags which he had loved.

Back in the valley, I found that a tall, slim girl was staying at the same cottage as my party. Her name, Fiona, held some of the haunting

Celtic sadness of the misty Western Isles. She had intriguing, un-fathomable eyes which quite failed to notice that I even existed. I was still more impressed when she and her girl friend, after a hard day on the mountains in heavy snow, set off gaily to meet friends at Pen-y-Gwryd, six miles away. Six miles! and I was aching in every muscle and could hardly move! Undoubtedly this was a girl who was not meant for me.

In spite of the obvious commonsense of this view, I sought her out back in London and, with other friends, she helped me paint my boat and sailed as one of the crew from Burnham-on-Crouch to Portsmouth on the first lap of the voyage to Plymouth. She learned how to steer and handle a ship and to climb the mast. And after recovering from sea sickness, she played her guitar. I was horrified to find that the stability of my smug, well-organized if rather complex, bachelor existence was beginning to be undermined by a new and disturbing emotion. Yet Fiona's feelings towards me remained entirely elusive.

All that Sunday at Cremyll the Mashfords went ahead with the mast. After stripping it of its metal fittings they sawed off the broken ends and bevelled each stump for about 5 feet. A new middle piece, made up of several planks, was planed to fit exactly, and that evening this rectangular middle section was clamped and glued into position between the halves of the old mast. Was the weather warm enough for the glue to set? This was now the vital question.

In the afternoon I restowed my spare Calor gas cylinders, which had started to bounce about on the cabin sole as the ship pitched. I screwed some eyebolts into the side of the bunks and lashed the cylinders down to them. This seemed to cure the trouble; but not for good, because some five thousand sea miles ahead I was to meet conditions that caused these eyebolts and lashings to prove totally inadequate.

On the morning of Monday, June 13th, I had to force myself to eat in the rush and excitement of the final preparations for departure. The new section, which had been scarphed into the mast, was now planed until round, then varnished, until the joint could hardly be seen. The mast, old sections and new, were held together by glue alone. The fittings were screwed and bolted on and new cross-trees, or spreaders, were made. It was the lower starboard cross-tree which had caused the accident. It had swivelled and snapped, leaving the mast without a major support to windward, so that it had immediately broken just above the spreader socket.

The wire and rope halyards that hoisted the sails had all been labelled before removal. In spite of this, there appeared to be hopeless confusion, for there were halyards to hoist the mainsail, the staysail and the genoa; one to raise the burgee or the racing flag, another for the spinnaker; and one for each of the spinnaker booms. Now they looked like a ball of demented knitting.

The tide was falling fast, too. Soon the ship would take the ground and then remain fixed for another twelve hours. And just as the keel was scraping the bottom, with workmen still tightening the last of the rigging screws, and while I hurriedly cleared the mainsail ready for hoisting, got into my P.V.C. smock and trousers and pulled on my rubber boots, Mashford's launch finally pulled us clear.

It was then a few minutes before noon G.M.T. on Monday the 13th.

"Monday by noon" Mr. Mashford had said she would be ready—and ready she was. At no time had he or his men indicated that there was anything unusual in their starting work at six o'clock on a Sunday morning or going on until midnight, and then setting-to at daybreak the next day. To talk to them you would have thought that this was all in a day's work. To meet these men had been a privilege. I not only owe them a debt I can never repay, but I learnt from them a new humility.

But now there was only room for one thought—to make sail again. A crowd of workmen were clustered on the pier head. A newspaper correspondent was standing among them. As the keel scraped free, while I was shipping the tiller and casting off lashings from the sails in much hurry and confusion, he called out with timing only surpassed by his tact:

"My readers would like to hear your last words, Doctor." Stung by the phrase, I shouted back furiously:

"I'm going to get to New York before those rascals drink all the beer and make love to all the women!"

A shocked hush had settled over the water, but the sails were up now and sheeted in. How good it was to feel the weight of the squalls in the canvas as *Cardinal Vertue* heeled over and raced before them through the smooth water down the Tamar and slipped silently out behind Drake's Island to head down Plymouth Sound towards the outer breakwater. Soon she felt the lift and scend of the living ocean out there beyond the headlands, and she became fully alive once more.

I had been encouraged so often since I had turned back ignominiously, that I thought that nothing more could happen to bolster my morale. I had done nothing to deserve the first send-off, but now I was getting another. Motoring alongside was a launch full of reporters, photographers and friends; the club commodore sailed past in his yacht; ferries, fishing boats and pleasure craft circled around, their crews waving and blowing their whistles in encouragement. How cheering it all was!

The day was overcast, with a strong wind blowing from the south-west, so that as I cleared the breakwater, *Cardinal Vertue* began to lay well over, pounding into the heavy seas.

Outside in Cawsand Bay a naval frigate lay at anchor; trim and seemingly disdainful. Suddenly, in a burst of colour, a string of flags broke from her yardarm. She was signalling me "Good luck". I waved back, deeply moved by their faith in a man who had none in himself at that moment, and carried on with a lighter heart adjusting the self-steering gear, tidying up the halyards on deck and putting things away down below.

Beyond the Eddystone the wind increased until I had to reef the mainsail. In *Cardinal Vertue* this is done by, first, wedging yourself on the steeply sloping deck by the mast, dressed in oilskins and rubber boots against the volleying spray. You slacken off the main halyard and rotate the boom with the reefing handle until the desired amount of sail is rolled around it. Then you slither back to the cockpit to slacken off the mainsheet so that the sail spills wind and you push the helm down to head the yacht up into the wind. Then back you go to the mast again and to set up the mainsail halyard hard. Now you can return to the cockpit and set the ship back on course. This takes seven minutes when all goes well; it has needed twenty minutes and up to nearly an hour on other occasions.

Soon the wind had risen to thirty miles an hour, the top of force 6, and was whining through the rigging. I rolled down another 4 feet of the mainsail, and this time I reefed the staysail, too.

The method of assessing the strength of the wind as different forces was introduced by Admiral Beaufort and is known as the Beaufort Scale. Forces 3 and 4 are good sailing breezes for the average yacht. Force 7 was originally described as "a wind in which a Ship of the Line could sail full-and-bye under all plain sail with the gun ports open, or a wind such as to cause a 30-foot fishing smack to heave to". Force 8 and above are gales.

When I streamed the patent log, which measures the distance a ship covers by means of a spinning rotator towed astern, the distant outline of the Eddystone lighthouse and the hills of England were just dipping below the swells and becoming invisible in the gathering dusk astern. I hoped fervently that this was the last that I should see of the land, at any rate for a long time.

I was still worried about the mast. I trembled with every creak of the timbers, as they strained to the tug of the rigging and the stress of the mast in the mast-step. I was shaking, sick with nerves and unable to eat. I noted wryly in the log-book that afternoon—

"It was a hero's send-off this morning, and now I lie in my bunk shivering with fear."

But the mast held, the ship tramped on her way south-west through the darkness and soon the moon could be glimpsed between ragged clouds, while the sea continued to get up, until sheets of spray rattled

against the sails and the cabin top, and breaking wave-crests thumped against the hull.

Once, through a momentary break in the clouds, like some visitor from a far-off time, I saw a barquentine under reduced canvas running eastward up Channel. Then the clouds came down again and she was hidden.

Midnight on June 14th found me anxiously going round the decks, checking over the halyards and the gear, and keeping a worried eye on the mast. I would try to rest, but soon worry would drive me on deck to inspect the mast and rigging yet again, before going below to lie down. I was too tense and excited to eat anything except some sweets and biscuits and to drink a little water, and later make a cup of coffee. I slept hardly at all that night.

At six o'clock next morning I was clearing seaweed from the deck, unrolling the mainsail and unreefing the staysail as the wind began to fall light, and *Cardinal Vertue*, still on the starboard tack, crept forward ever more slowly.

Just before midday I took a meridian altitude of the sun on the sextant. I had to look up the method in my text-book, because I had never tried it before. In clear weather this is an easy way to find the latitude. You do not need the exact time. A little before noon, you take readings of the sun's altitude at short intervals, until it no longer rises but seems to hang stationary for some minutes and then begins to sink, so that the altitude readings no longer increase but become less. The highest figure obtained is used, and a simple calculation gives the latitude of the ship.

That afternoon the wind was becoming lighter and lighter. Several ships and some fishing boats passed in the distance. I washed and opened up all the hatches to air the ship. Gradually it fell calm, and as the afternoon wore on, the sails, now uncontrolled by the force of the wind, began to slat violently as the ship rolled in the heavy swell.

This was the first of the many frustrating calms I was to meet. For hours, no matter how tight the boom was pulled in by the sheet, there would be the shrill squeak of the blocks as the boom slammed over a fraction of an inch, and the swish, swish of the sail as it was thrown first to one side then to the other. These are the most irritating sounds that a seaman ever has to hear.

I started to make a recording on the tape-recorder I had been lent, describing the start, the repairs and second start, and when I played it back months later I could hear the frightened, tremulous note in my voice. That afternoon I had my first cooked meal at sea—eggs and bacon, bread and butter and coffee. I concluded the recording with the words:

"The sun has just sunk into the Western Ocean. The sky foretells plenty of wind."

June 15th. By midnight the sails began to stir again. It was a calm clear night. So good was the visibility that I could see the loom of the lights on Ushant and Ile Vierge off the French coast, and when looking astern, could count the beams from the Lizard. The Lizard and Ushant are ninety miles apart. It was not so pleasant, when I took a bearing on these lights, to find that I had been swept well back by the tide while I had been becalmed in the afternoon. Slowly the wind increased that night and during the next day. Again I had to reef and to keep adjusting the self-steering gear to cope with the variable winds.

As yet I had not found my sea legs. I was falling about heavily each time the ship lurched and I tried to move, and now I was cut and bruised all over. Towards evening several seas burst across the deck soaking me through gaps in my oilskins. As *Cardinal Vertue* pitched and rolled, I looked up to see a Blue Star steamer going past, as steady as if she were sailing over a lake. Why does one ever go to sea in small boats, I wondered? Gradually in the evening the mist closed down becoming thicker and thicker. The position line I had obtained that afternoon was to be the last for four days.

Each of the five competitors in the race had designed a self-steering gear, or automatic helmsman, to keep his yacht on a constant course in relation to the wind.

Each of us had our own ideas and we had the experience of others to guide us. Michael Henderson had tried vane-steering on several light-displacement craft in the Solent and Channel; Lewis King had made one for his *Jeanne Matilde* to use on his seventeen thousand miles voyage from Singapore to England. It had worked quite well until an inquisitive steamer passed too close and knocked it into the South Atlantic. Ian Major's *Buttercup* used a most successful vane on his Atlantic crossing, and Valentine Howells had made one for a voyage to Spain the summer before our race.

However, none of these was the originator of the method. Three months before the race I had been invited to study at the "source".

"Is that *the* Doctor Lewis, the famous physician?" a voice on the telephone had asked.

"Oh, go away, Francis. I'm busy," I had replied peevishly.

"David, come with me to the Round Pond, Kensington, on Sunday to see how to make a self-steering gear properly! Those model yacht chaps really know how to sail. I go there each Sunday to get hints."

Francis Chichester was right, of course; the model makers first thought of this idea.

My own vane was of the trim tab or servo rudder type and its design and working principle are described in Appendix Two. Its design owes much to several people, especially Val Howells, but its success I maintain, is largely attributable to its true personality—the prim Kiwi painted upon it and watching over it!

Exchanging information about such potentially race-winning gadgets was typical of the spirit of the competitors in this unique race. On Val's good advice I discarded my first ideas on a steering device. Blondie sent round a letter in March:

"I will offer any help I can with vane gears, and *if* you are using a

1. A pre-race trial of *Cardinal Vertue's* self-steering gear.

2. Looking down on *Cardinal Vertue*'s reinforced doghouse and self-draining cockpit.

trim tab system, and *if* you are getting oversteering effects, I should be happy to let you study *Jester's* linkage. . . ."

For though we were racing against each other, we were also knit in fellowship in face of our common antagonist, the Western Ocean.

June 16th. Out of the shimmering fog, long slow rollers came from the south-west, like moving downs and pastures of the sea. They had travelled unhindered three thousand miles from America. I washed and shaved; usually I managed to shave every second or third day. After every meal I tried to wash up at once, having long ago discovered that if one leaves so much as a greasy knife, it will butter the whole cabin in an instant. Soon I was almost becalmed and for the first time for forty-four hours I was able to take off my P.V.C. smock, waterproof trousers, safety-belt and rubber boots.

I got out the tape-recorder on which Fiona had recorded some songs, both her own and others from gramophone records. Everything aboard reminded me of my friends. The tape-recorder belonged to Garth and Leslie Harvey. A bundle of burgees had been given by Arnold Greenwood of The Little Ship Club, Cecily's kiwi flag flew at the masthead; there was Ken's echo-sounder, Herbert's radio and Wilfred's compass—or rather Garth's compass that Wilfred had altered for me. Everywhere I looked there were signs of people's kindness: notes on tins and lists of food which Cecily had prepared. I was oppressed by the knowledge that I had not even thanked one of them. I had been so irritable on the morning of the 11th and now I wrote in my log-book that I had better realize I would have no friends at all on my return, and that I did not deserve any either!

During the night the fog became very thick and damp and the first dismal hoots of ships' foghorns became audible. The sounds came closer, until I had to put on my heavy clothing and safety-belt again and clamber out into the cockpit to blow hopefully on a tiny hooter until the invisible ship had passed. Everything was dripping in the heavy banks of fog. At intervals all through the night I listened and peered anxiously for passing ships. I was using the electric navigation lights at this stage of the voyage and also relying on any big ship's radar to pick up my 14-foot metal spinnaker pole which hung down the mast. I had a rather frail radar reflector as well, but it seemed wise to conserve this until later for the Grand Banks of Newfoundland, usually the foggiest sea area in the world.

June 17th. There was no possibility of getting a sight of the sun during these days, but with the radio direction-finder I was able to obtain the bearing of a station at Ploneis in the North of France and another of Mizzen Head in the West of Ireland. I found that I was seventy miles south and a little west of the Fastnet Rock, off Ireland, with about thirty-five miles to go until I was clear of the west of Ireland altogether and out in the open Atlantic. During the night I had crossed the main shipping lanes, so the traffic was now to my port side.

Visibility was a little better in the afternoon so I slept for two hours without my P.V.C. suit and trousers. I decided, however, that for the whole voyage I would wear my safety-belt before laying down to sleep, in case I was suddenly awakened to deal with some emergency on deck. For this was the time when reflexes would be sluggish. It would be no use regretting the one false step during that agonizing last swim! To slip over the side of a yacht steering itself is equivalent to stepping out of an aircraft without a parachute. Any carelessness about this would be inexcusable.

I was awakened that afternoon by the sails slatting violently. The ship had gybed in a wind too light to work the vane, was caught aback, and was now "calling for help". To get her on course again in these circumstances was one of the few things a self-steering vane could not do by itself. *Cardinal Vertue* and her wind vane were both so efficient that I felt less redundant now that I had something to do. As I brought the ship on course I looked alongside to see a shark about $3\frac{1}{2}$ feet long swimming quite near.

Perhaps I should have tested his behaviour with the shark repellent we had been given, but he looked such a friendly little fellow and I was afraid it would work. I did not want him to go away for he made me feel that now we were really at sea, like the people who sail exotic oceans such as the South Pacific. To my disappointment, after circling the ship once or twice, he swam away to the westward.

At the end of a short calm the wind came in from astern so that for the first time I was able to lay the correct course.

It was still foggy, still no sight of the sun, but as the ship ran on, my mood began to lighten and as I looked back out of the cabin at the kiwi painted on the self-steering vane, I felt that he, too, was developing something of a happier personality.

A kiwi is a particularly appropriate mascot for a ship called *Cardinal Vertue*. Not only is he our New Zealand national bird but he has no wings and does not indulge in stupid pastimes, like floating on the sea, or flying, or anything else so silly. Moreover, the male bird has so many domestic virtues; he sits on the huge egg to incubate it; then he feeds and takes care of the young. An admirable creature!

At first he did not know quite what was happening. When the wind was rising and the clouds went scudding by, he used to peer anxiously aloft as if to say:

"Oh dear, whatever next!"—"And the egg, too! However did that get there?"

Now he had an air of smug efficiency! At least he was watching what was happening, and was steering the ship. He looked more confident, too, as if he had realized, at last, that kiwis *should* go to sea.

June 18th. We went on through thick fog through the night of the 17th–18th. By two o'clock in the morning the wind had veered a little so I decided to try out my twin headsails. In the damp mist and the dark, setting them was a slow, dismal job. The wet ropes took on a malicious life of their own, tangling themselves in coils. It took me fourteen minutes to undo one single topping-lift that had been too neatly coiled up by a friend in Plymouth! As I sat struggling with them in pitch darkness on the dripping deck, a foghorn began to blare away somewhere ahead.

Later during the morning of the 18th the wind dropped to a light breeze so that I had to steer. Then the wind backed and I had to change sail again. This time I was able to make a quicker change. For an hour I sat at the tiller composing doubtful ditties about my friends until, as the wind strengthened once more, I could go below and leave *Cardinal Vertue* to herself. Soon it fell a flat calm, the sea undulating in great rollers, a beautiful deep blue, as well it might be, for there were two miles of water under the keel.

But I had no eyes for the beauty of the blue sea nor for the tiny Portuguese men-of-war that seemed to appear by magic every time the wind dropped. Always in these calms a profound depression dominated me. Hour after hour the ship would wallow helplessly in the swell, rolling 20 degrees each way. There was a vicious brutality in the slap, slap, slap of the sails, something of the shock of a hand being slapped to and fro across a face, and on it would go, on and on.

Light airs can be even more trying than calms. With bare steerage way the ship begins to move, then promptly throws herself about. You have to gybe her around on to her course again. In a few moments she is aback once more. Then she is stationary. You are barely moving, yet you cannot leave the tiller. You get up another headsail; try to steer a course; five minutes later the wind peters out again. Sometimes after half an hour's work you come upon the same piece of paper which you threw over the side an hour ago, drifting ahead of you.

At the beginning of each calm I found it very difficult to get down to work. I had not the heart to do any of the jobs that needed doing. But until I started working, and this needed a great effort, it was impossible to overcome my depression.

So now to occupy my mind I plotted the last known position (June 8th) of the ice off Newfoundland. There seemed to be rather less of it than usual. However, the icebergs, which the spring thaw had released from the Polar pack, were being carried by the Labrador current over thousands of square miles of sea, and they could have drifted almost anywhere by the time I passed that way. It was certain that I would have to pass for days, probably weeks, through the area studded with bergs and shrouded with fog.

After this I washed handkerchiefs, shirts, and underclothes, then stripped down in the cockpit and washed myself all over. Next I examined the rigging for signs of chafe.

At 8 p.m. the wind came in from the starboard quarter and *Cardinal Vertue* began to run swiftly and silently, into the mist and gathering darkness, smoothly breasting the long swells. At least we were moving again, but what of the others, I thought dismally? Hundreds and hundreds of miles ahead and surely well out of this damned anticyclone with its calms.

Still, for the moment, hard work had proved an antidote to the calm weather depression and the main steamer lanes of the Western Approaches now lay astern. The nervous tension of the last few days was relaxing and suddenly the realization burst upon me that at last I was free from all the complex problems of those months of preparation ashore, and could give myself up to that peace and confidence that the great oceans and high mountains bestow upon those who go upon them.

The adventure, which had for so long been a distant dream, had now begun. Although I was to have cause to know fear, to experience thirst, frustration and bitter disappointment, the unsettled anxious misgivings of the first days at sea were never to return again. Though in every calm I was frantic with helpless irritation, the mood passed when the wind returned.

I slept soundly that night although I had to get up repeatedly between midnight and dawn to adjust the wind-vane to the variable easterlies. Twice while I was in the cockpit, ships' lights appeared in the distance, through momentary breaks in the fog.

On June 19th sunlight came filtering through a thin layer of mist to warm the ship as she rolled along. The air temperature was 68°F. Dressed modestly in just my safety-belt I took the opportunity to open up every locker and hatch to air the ship until the mist again closed down, damp and clammy in the late afternoon. I was happy and relaxed and enjoying the most wonderful holiday. I remembered with horror my irritability and pettiness.

By noon on June 20th I had been a whole week at sea. Now, at last, after four days the fog lifted. A sun sight gave a position line passing within two miles of the estimated position. But I had to wait another day for a further sight by which to fix my position exactly. The estimated position is the calculated position based on the patent log readings, the estimated set and drift of the current, leeway and the compass courses sailed.

Both sight and estimation put me about four hundred and thirty-six nautical miles from Plymouth. The best days' run (from noon to noon) had been only eighty-six miles and the worst twenty-seven. There had been four days and six hours of continuous fog and mist.

I had hoped to make much better time than this, but at least I was on the shortest route to New York, west of Southern Ireland now and passing about thirteen hundred miles north of the Canary Islands. It was not so much the contrary winds that had delayed me. I had expected them; indeed for the last twenty-six hours a following wind had enabled me to set the spinnaker, a huge balloon sail of nylon.

But on four days there had been nine unspeakable hours with no wind whatsoever; many more hours when there had been light airs and zephyrs. These were conditions against which I had no weapon. But in spite of this, the fogs and contrary winds, the week had brought peace of mind. Now, at last, the fear of another disaster to the mast, whenever it creaked, had partly receded, although it was to remain a worry for another month until the scarphed "stick" had proved itself in test by storm.

Before me lay one problem only—how best to handle my craft so that she made the fastest possible progress westward. I was happy now with a renewed sense of humour and a quickening feeling of adventure as we pushed further westward. Between the calms I felt at one with the sea and the sky and even with the grey mist. These were antagonists with which I could join battle using my brains and energy to the full, as befits a man faced with worthy foes. For the vast elements are not hostile or unkind, they are too big and aloof for petty spite.

I was eating properly for the first time for a week; I was sleeping better. But each night I would dream; and the characters in the dreams were always the same—Blondie Hasler, Francis Chichester and Val Howells. Sometimes we were sailing or racing against each other; while on other occasions they were actors in some bizarre dream drama; but until I reached New York all my dreams centred on these three men, the sea, and often the race.

3

ORDEAL BY CALM

The winds have not read
the American Pilot Charts.
—H. G. HASLER

JUNE 21st. A night and morning of calm. Brief panic ensued when a sun sight gave a position line through County Cork, a result which conflicted with the heaving ocean all around! A check showed that I had logged ten minutes to ten o'clock as 10.50 a.m. instead of 9.50. Faith in my navigation was restored.

Whenever the weather was clear I took a morning sight once the sun was over 20 degrees above the horizon, another about midday and a third in the afternoon. The noon sight gave a position line approximating to latitude and the others to longitude. Alternatively, I would take only two sights at a sufficient interval of time to give position lines with a good cut.

I was at last mastering the knack of wedging my hips in the main hatchway so that my trunk remained upright and the sextant could be held steady, while the ship rolled and pitched under me and my body swayed to the sea's rhythm. A lightning glance at the wrist-watch the moment the sun's reflection touched the horizon, then I would clamber laboriously below, clinging on with one hand and guarding the sextant from harm as I was buffeted in the companionway. Next, I would note down the time and the sextant reading, comparing the wrist-watch with the deck-watch that rested in its nest of National Health Service cotton wool on a special shelf. I now knew it gained two seconds a day. It was as well that this error remained regular as the B.B.C. time signals were becoming very faint.

Bracing myself firmly into position beside the chart table with the Nautical Almanac and Admiralty Tables beside me, I worked out the sight in about twelve minutes, plotting the resulting position line on the chart in use.

Perhaps I am making heavy weather of this description; but I had

27

only learnt navigation by attending fortnightly evening classes at the Little Ship Club during the winter. Not the brightest of pupils, I soon gave up trying to learn star or moon sights, concentrating solely on the sun. Nor did I sit for the examination that concluded the lectures, for I did not know enough to pass and failure would have further lowered my already shaky morale. Best, I thought, to learn one simple routine so thoroughly that when sick and frightened and buffeted by giant seas, I could pass the examination that would be set by the grim Atlantic.

Besides, a sailor can be too fussy about details. Joshua Slocum, the first man to sail alone round the world, used a kitchen clock as his chronometer. When it stopped he boiled it in oil. An unsolved riddle is why it worked again! Still earlier, when the 70-foot double canoe *Tainui* sailed from Tahiti on the fourth night of December 1350, all that Taikehu had to guide him—Taikehu who "had charge of the great paddle Huahuaterangi"—were directions handed down two hundred years before by Kupe, The Navigator. "Steer a little to the left of the setting sun in December and you will reach Aotea-roa, the Land of the Long White Cloud." And reach New Zealand the *Tainui* Maoris did— over two thousand miles of open ocean, in company with the canoes *Tokomaru, Takatimu, Aotea* and *Arawa*.

How true a seafaring spirit that old Viking helmsman, Bard, showed, too, when, a thousand years ago, he led a party of young men from Iceland towards Norway. The Saga tells: "They got so strong a wind from the north that they were driven south into the main; and so much mist that they could not tell where they were driving, and they were out a long while." When a ground swell warned them of nearby land the old man was asked where they were. He answered this silly question with dignity:

"Many lands there are which we might have hit with the weather we have had—the Orkneys or Scotland or Ireland."

They rowed on to recognize the north coast of Scotland.

For hours *Cardinal Vertue* turned slow circles, inert and without life; not even a zephyr stirred. Then, at last, the sea's surface crinkled, changing from glossy to matt as the first ruffling breeze breathed out of the south.

That sunny afternoon, while the yacht was running her westing down, I described on the tape-recorder the rules which trial and error had now taught me:

"First, I must keep the ship sailing as fast as possible on the right course; that is, on the shortest route between my position and New York.

"Then, equipment needs to be maintained in good order; I must never let important things go by the board, yet not exhaust myself by trying to do everything: for instance, when the genoa tore the other day, I mended it as soon as it was dry, without waiting until it was needed again.

"I pump the bilges several times a day to stop water sloshing up behind the bunks at every roll; run the engine every day to charge the battery; keep stock of water and provisions; turn off the Calor gas cylinder *always* after use; write up the logs regularly; and often make notes of tasks still to be done.

"But I do not batten down everything at night. I think one can get into an unnecessary panic about the darkness. It is just the same as day; one should be ready to reduce or change sail, or alter course, and if everything is in its proper place, halyards always on the same cleats for instance, work is easy in the dark.

"Only in bad weather do I lash down the forehatch, fit the wash-boards and make all secure below.

"Similarly, I must be careful not to make a fetish of the safety-belt. A man could become afraid to move without clipping the thing on, and then when he was going from one part of the deck to another and had to unclip it, he could lose his balance and go over. I am well aware that the fundamental rule of single-handed sailing is that one stays with the ship. One must stay aboard, but the prerequisites for doing this are alertness, keen balance, quickness and being generally at home with the boat.

"Not that I neglect the belt. I am now sitting in the cockpit in the sunshine wearing nothing else. We are making three knots and I might have to adjust the vane or go forward, If so, I will clip the belt to something—for I do not think I could swim at this speed!"

The next two days were mainly notable for enteritis contracted through eating the last of my bacon when it had already become mouldy and unsavoury. *Cardinal Vertue* and the wind vane made the best progress they could against light unfavourable winds while the skipper was otherwise occupied.

Then on June 23rd "mare's tails" of cirrus cloud, and a grey, fibrous veil of alto-stratus, began to spread over the sky from the westward. The north-west wind backed into the south; the barometer began to fall.

As I was now outside the sea areas included in the B.B.C.'s weather bulletins (I could hardly hear the radio anyway) I had to do my own forecasting. This was great fun. One of my main sources of information was the section on meteorology that forms part of the introduction to every *Admiralty Pilot*.

In the North Atlantic low pressure areas, or depressions, move towards Europe from Canada. Most pass north of British latitudes. The sequence of events is as follows: high cloud spreads, perhaps forming a "halo" around sun or moon—the "mackerel sky and mare's tails" that made "tall ships carry low sails", of the old sailor's rhyme.

The glass falls and the wind backs towards the south. Then, as the sky becomes overcast, the wind increases; low ragged clouds scud by; rain falls; and the wind veers. When the warm front passes there is a sudden further veer to SW or WSW. Eventually the cold front goes by, accompanied by another abrupt veer in the wind and often by vicious line squalls. The glass begins to rise; the air becomes colder; and the sky clears. The wind, which is now from west or north-west, may blow still harder until the whole system has passed by.

"Lows" are caused by cold Polar air displacing warmer air masses. The winds may be moderate, but depressions are also breeding grounds for gales.

I have written at length about the weather because at sea you live with it; your tactics are dictated by it; you must learn its laws or it may destroy you. So, close to nature, did our ancestors live. True, we have not their belief that we can influence natural forces—Slocum once remarked that he had found praying for a favourable change of wind to be more effective where winds were naturally variable than in the steady Trades. But we can use the accumulated skill and knowledge of centuries to live safely among the winds of heaven.

The sky signs on June 23rd did not lie. The wind gradually veered until I could no longer lay my westerly course, but was forced north on the port tack through damp mist, light rain and overcast; and soon the wind strengthened. I had picked up the mast winch handle to go on deck and reef, but the wind fell right away, and the sea suddenly became "spiky" as little pyramidal waves splashed upward, released from the power which had moulded them into orderly shapes.

When the wind came in again it blew from farther west. Several times this was repeated. Sometimes I did have to reef, once to roll the mainsail right down and change to the tiny No. 3 staysail. Then, as the wind died down before changing to its new direction, the mainsail would have to be unrolled again. The warm front passed in the early morning hours of the 24th, after which I could sail no better course than north-west.

In a bleak dawn the sharply veering squall of the cold front pressed *Cardinal Vertue* hard over. I came about on to the starboard tack which was now the most favourable, but south-west was the nearest she could lie to the proper westerly course.

Gradually the depression passed north, leaving the glass high and the wind dropping. I had only made forty-two miles westward during the past twenty-four hours, at the cost of such frequent changes in course and alterations in sail area that I had had no sleep.

But I would far rather fight to windward than see the glass rise from 1,015 mb to 1,022, 1,024, 1,030, and the sky turn a clear blue, while the sea changed from grey-green to indigo and then became an undulating sheet of burnished copper. *Cardinal Vertue* floated motionless.

"In the middle of an anticyclone," I said on the tape-recorder next morning, the 25th. "I wish to God it would change, but those are all fair weather clouds on the horizon. I have been becalmed since yesterday, I know I am not being very positive about this but I am so depressed. Those damned Portuguese men-of-war are going faster than I am.

"I must try to fight this demoralization that obsesses me because I'm not getting anywhere; give myself a mental kick; make every effort to use each tiny puff of wind to the best advantage.

"I will try to forget how big the ocean is, and how small are the distances between the crosses marked on my chart each noon. I know this is a small ocean compared with the Indian Ocean or the Pacific, but it does seem unnecessarily large to me.

"I find it too depressing to read the accounts of two pioneers of this crossing, Graham in 1934 or Hamilton twenty years later. Their positions moved steadily westward—and that is a damned sight more than mine are doing! I have been at work, trying to lighten my mood by washing clothes and myself; not that I am inordinately clean but it does pay to keep one's skin healthy at sea. Then I checked food and stores.

"The day before the race Cicely asked what I was taking.

" 'Only the basic dehydrated food, I haven't had time to think of anything else,' I had replied. 'Can you go into Plymouth today and

31

buy me six weeks' supplies?' She did it too! But of course there had to be shortages. I have just discovered that I have already used two-thirds of the matches aboard, so will ration strictly until I am farther over. I have decided to use no more than one match a day. This will allow one hot meal and drink until I have built up a reserve stock. No real hardship as the weather is still warm.

"I did not bring enough matches, but to make up for this deficiency I *did* buy a 'gale cheater', better called a 'spoil sport machine'. This hand-held indicator records the wind velocity in miles per hour. The actual reading has to be corrected by adding or subtracting the ship's speed and then by adding 30 per cent. to obtain the corrected wind speed at 33 feet above sea level. All wind speed figures I am giving here are for corrected velocities.

"I am quite sure that without it I would already have been through a couple of gales; *at least* force 8! Unfortunately, with the gadget I knew they were only force 6 winds, so they had to be logged accordingly. I warn other yachtsmen not to take any wind speed device with them: it completely spoils your entries—and the epic stories to be told on return."

But that morning no indicator was necessary in the still lifeless air.

By 2.0 p.m. it no longer needed a forced effort to be of good cheer. I opened the tape-recorder again and exclaimed:

"It is exciting—no, not exciting exactly—exhilarating—a wonderful feeling of freedom! Can you hear the water rushing by as I hold the microphone over the side? Yes; the ship is running. The spinnaker has been up and drawing for half an hour now; blue sea, blue sky with scattered cumulus clouds; and I'm sitting naked in the cockpit with a large gin. Once a shower of little fish came spraying into the air and I thought for a moment that I must be in the tropics among the flying fish. Where are the whales and other exciting sea animals one reads about? So far they are being coy.

"There is one snag; I want to charge the battery but cannot start the engine. Two hours' work has been of no avail, but I will try again later. If it refuses to go for the rest of the voyage it means, at worst, no navigation lights (except for short periods in emergencies), no cabin lights, no radio transmitter or spare receiver, no compass light; I shall have to use the torch for that.

"Possibly if I hang the paraffin riding light in the cabin, when I have caught up with matches, I may still be able to read. We are south of the shipping lanes now; just as well as we are without navigation lights;

have been extravagant leaving them on while I slept. If I can keep away from the steamers I should be all right." I was not being pessimistic. The engine did not run again.

The easterly wind steadily increased. At 10 p.m. after I had lowered the spinnaker, *Cardinal Vertue* continued to run at six knots by the patent log, nearly her maximum speed under mainsail alone. Soon I was rolling down 3 feet of the mainsail, but in under an hour I had to close-reef. It was a wonderful sail, tearing away through the darkness leaving a frothing wake, with the seas foaming up alongside.

By 4 a.m. on June 26th I was tired after this exhilarating but strenuous night. The ship would steer herself for about fifteen minutes until a sea breaking against her quarter would slew her round until she broached-to and lay in the troughs of the waves. The wind-vane could not get her back on course so I would clamber out, cursing, and push the helm up.

It was blowing a full gale, force 8, and I lowered all sail, though this was quite unnecessary. *Cardinal Vertue* would have sailed perfectly well under the full staysail.

But the sea and sky were grey and brooding. Great smoking combers came rolling out of the murk to windward. Every now and then one would burst against the ship, throwing her over 40 degrees. The seas, dotted with breaking crests, looked as soft as cotton wool—but how solid they felt as they roared down on the little ship to burst against her.

I pumped the bilge, then wrote in my diary:

"This was to have been a tape-recording but as I laid the machine tenderly in the lee bunk, the ship crashed over on her side and it shot smartly across the cabin. Now it will not work.

"My first gale! Even if it is only a small one, it *is* the first. I am pleased and excited. I was becoming worried, fearing I might be the only person to sail this stretch of ocean without one, as well as making the slowest passage on record. At daylight a fair-sized shark was flopping about near the surface, tail and fin out, brown shadow close beneath."

But the exhilaration passed as tiredness took hold and I became more damp and chilled and bruised all over.

The pitching and rolling of a small ship at sea is generally such that you must either hold on continually with one hand, or brace yourself securely if you have to use both. Even to make a mug of coffee, I would first place coffee, milk, sugar, mug and spoon on the lee side of the cabin sole, then wedge myself on the floorboards beside them. Before I stood up again the ingredients had to be safe in their locker and the mug firmly jammed in another. I could then light the gas. For weeks your home is rolling and pitching violently, and often being dropped several feet with disconcerting abruptness.

But as the motion of a yacht at sea compares with the stillness of a house on shore, so is the fearful tossing about in a gale to normal ocean sailing. You try to eliminate unnecessary effort, but this is sometimes false economy. The log notes laconically how I tried to avoid going out into the cockpit, or making the acrobatic journey forward to "the heads", using the washing-up bowl instead. I was trying to lift it outside between the washboards and spray hood when a sea threw the ship on her beam ends, and over me it went!

Before midday I had set the reefed staysail, and, still grossly under-canvased, was running down my westing over huge swells in a confused sea. The wind decreased until at 7 p.m. I was able to cook baked beans and dehydrated stew with mugs of coffee, still keeping to the ration of one match a day. Then I repaired a rent in my P.V.C. trousers and changed my damp clothes.

Next day at noon I had been two weeks out and was half-way between Plymouth and Cape Race, Newfoundland. Far south lay the Azores and hundreds of miles to the northward I had just cleared the longitude of Iceland. I celebrated with the last of my half-bottle of gin.

"On these days of middle passage," I wrote, "it requires great mental effort to keep up keenness and make it an unbreakable rule to run out westing. The lesson of the previous day's blow is clear. I hoisted the mainsail much too late today. Yesterday, I need never have lowered the staysail. So far I have generally been about right when to shorten sail, but very slow indeed in realizing it is time to make sail again. I must watch this carefully and stop fussing over the mast.

"Where are my companions—rivals? I think of them a lot. They must be a hell of a long way ahead. I hope they haven't had the same calms I have had; but I am human enough to hope that they are not too far ahead. I would like them still to be in New York when I get there."

On that day, June 27th, Francis Chichester, I learnt later, was actually three hundred and seventy-five miles west-south-west of me, his position being 48° 30' N, 34° 08' W, and mine 50° 10' N, 25° 10' W. Two days before, a severe gale had overtaken him with scant warning. He was westward of, but near to, the centre of a low-pressure system, while I was at its eastern margin. On June 25th, according to the daily weather reports of the British Meteorological Office, a vessel reported winds of force 8, and on the 26th another ship, on the eastern outskirts of the disturbance about one hundred and thirty miles to the west of me, reported winds of forty-seven knots (force 9). Francis found the gale to be stronger still, while I was experiencing my first force 8 blow that morning.

I think my readings of wind velocity were accurate, as they were logged with regard to the state and appearance of the sea and not merely the indicator reading. The instrument was often washed out with fresh water as it repeatedly became clogged with spray. Subsequent comparison of my estimates of wind velocity with ocean weather ship reports, on the two occasions when I experienced gales in their vicinity, showed a close correlation between the figures.

Francis Chichester had spent more than five hours stripping the huge sails from *Gipsy Moth III* before she was running under bare poles. Her mainsail and genoa each measure 380 square feet compared with the 180 of my mainsail, and 230 of my genoa, and Hasler's 240 square foot single Chinese lug-sail. (Conventional Folkboats, such as Val Howells' *Eira*, carry a total of 250 square feet in mainsail and headsail.) *Eira* has 380 square feet when carrying her masthead genoa.

"The din was appalling," Chichester wrote of that gale. "A high-pitched screech dominating everything, spray peppering everywhere and seas hitting periodically with the bonk of a big drum."

To slow down his ship, he shackled a motor tyre on to the anchor chain, which he payed out over the stern, together with twenty fathoms of 2½-inch warp. He filled a tin with oil, punctured it and hung it amidships. The anchor chain left a white wake behind.

June 28th found a battered but indomitable Francis repairing his self-steering gear as the wind fell below gale force.

On the same date Blondie Hasler's *Jester* was at 56° 12' N, 36° 50' W, south-east of Greenland, four hundred and fifty miles north-west of my position. He had passed the half-way mark between the continents and wrote: "Rather restless, tried to do some writing but found it hard to concentrate—partly because *Jester* is doing five knots through fog."

Hasler's log makes his passage sound easy, but he once admitted that it was "A little upsetting to see your mast waving to and fro". Rather an understatement, as his mast was completely unstayed. On the 25th he wrote: "Depressed . . . all sorts of doubts about my rig, provisions and time needed to get to New York. I dispelled this feeling in the afternoon by doing some work aboard."

By this time his rig had really been proved by a three-day gale. On the 26th the weather had moderated enough for him to inspect his ship and find all well. His morale "soared" that day.

I hope I am not picturing Hasler as some iron man, brave only because he fails to notice danger. True, unlike myself, he did not once tick "Very scared" in his medical log. But his courage is that of a bold imaginative mind. Both his wartime exploits and his success in ocean racing stem from planning and logical deduction, leading to definite decision and self-control over fear.

I had never known him so happy and relaxed as at Plymouth, with the enterprise which he had launched about to begin. The day I arrived he had taken me aside:

"David, I have had a little luck and made some money unexpectedly. How are you fixed for dollars? Let me lend you $200 to help out in New York."

There are not many men so ready to share good fortune with their friends. Luckily I was confident by then of getting away without a warrant being nailed to the mast. Not that I was solvent. Two years would be about the minimum to pay for the expenses incurred in the race. But that didn't matter so long as I could take part. So I refused Blondie's offer, as I had $30 of my own for the other side.

"Val has been the sensible one," I said. "He has a metal mast so that no one can nail a warrant to it and stop him sailing." We gazed in silent envy at this evidence of Howell's foresight.

By now, June 27th, Val, who was taking the intermediate route, was nearing the Azores. He completed his first thousand miles that day. I had done eight hundred and thirty, but my route was shorter. "My mind is boggling at the idea of spending another five weeks in this manner . . . feel dirty, have nearly saved enough water for another bath . . . have finished all the reading matter, very very bored," he wrote.

The moment of truth for Val and his metal mast was to come later when he found a second use for it. He was north-east of Bermuda sailing well-reefed through a belt of squalls. None appeared to be moving his way so he went below. Suddenly *Eira* was laid flat by the wind, her mast and sails pressed into the sea. Only the raised cabin coamings prevented her from filling through the main companion hatch and sinking like a stone.

3. (*Above*) *Cardinal Vertue* under mainsail and genoa.

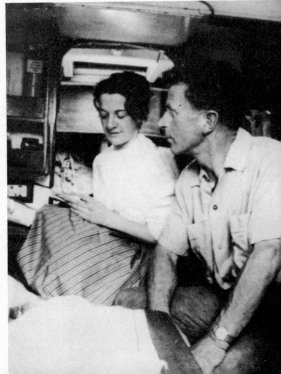

4. (*Right*) Looking forward in the cabin. David Lewis with Fiona.

5. (*Left*) "I would climb the mast . . . to become accustomed to the effort and balance involved . . . in case this proved necessary at sea."

6. (*Below*) The author in the pulpit of *Cardinal Vertue* a fortnight before the race.

"It was hard getting on deck and working my way along to the mast to get the sails down," Howells said afterwards. Considering that the deck was vertical, no one would doubt this.

When at last *Eira* was upright again he wondered how long it had all taken and glanced down at his wrist-watch-chronometer to find it had disappeared during those desperate minutes. He was left without means of finding his longditude and so decided to run his westing down in the latitude of Bermuda.

Jean Lacombe had started on June 16th, and by the 27th was in the latitude of Cape Finisterre, heading towards the Azores.

How had we become so scattered? The course of the Single-handed Transatlantic Race had been laconically laid down in the sailing instructions as, "Cross the starting line from West to East. Leave the Melampus Buoy to starboard, thence to New York by any route." The finish was at the Ambrose Light Vessel in the approaches to New York harbour. There was, therefore, a good deal of scope for the strategic planning of one's route.

We had two main choices; southern or trade wind, and the more northerly direct great circle route. There were also two variations, the intermediate way and the far north track.

We had pored over "Ocean Passages of the World"; the Admiralty chart of sailing ship routes, the monthly Pilot Charts, which contain detailed information about winds, currents, drift ice, fog, etc.; and over the accounts of other seamen.

When I first went to see Hasler, it was clear that we both favoured some variant of the northern route. I preferred the great circle; Hasler, impressed by accounts of 19th-century sailing-ship masters who found they could reach New York quicker from the Clyde than from Falmouth, intended to sail to the north of the shortest track.

At that time we insisted our interest in the race was purely theoretical. I had written to him "On behalf of friends who were interested," and he was "Most unlikely" to enter himself. But as we were saying good-bye at the station, after a discussion over a pint or two of beer, Blondie exclaimed:

"Well at least there will be two of us in this damned race, even if we are the only ones!"

But soon he 'phoned me about Francis Chichester. "The chap who flew the Tasman sea alone in a little seaplane and taught himself navigation to find two tiny islands on the way—then developed the methods the pathfinder pilots used during the war. He is interested."

Chichester insisted that he was not really serious about the race, so I was amused to see that "purely by chance" he had in his office about twenty pounds worth of charts which, "by a most fortunate coincidence, happened to cover the course of the race". Here was the man who, in stubborn refusal to accept defeat, had rebuilt his wrecked seaplane on a Pacific island during his historic New Zealand-Australia flight thirty years before. This same tenacity and singleness of purpose had helped him recover from a lung abscess the previous year.

Later we met Val Howells, the huge black-bearded Welshman who had sailed alone to Spain in preparation for his Atlantic crossing. Cuba was in the news just then, and little boys had followed him through the streets of San Sebastian, shouting, "*Ole, Fidelito Castro!*" Val rather favoured the intermediate route.

Jean Lacombe was the only one of us who "knew the way", from his previous crossing. He too, preferred this route.

The shortest way from Plymouth to New York without crossing over land is by sailing a great circle from Land's End to the tip of Newfoundland, roughly two thousand miles, thence parallel with the Canadian and American coasts, west-south-westwards for a little over a thousand miles to the Ambrose Light off New York. A great circle is the shortest distance between two points on a globe and in this case the course is a shade north of west from the Lizard to a position 51° N 20° W, then curves gently south to Cape Race, Newfoundland.

The intermediate route taken by Humphrey Barton in *Vertue XXXV* is some three thousand, six hundred and sixty-nine miles, passing a hundred miles north of the Azores and about two hundred miles north of Bermuda. In their passage from Falmouth to New York in forty-seven days, he and Kevin O'Riordan averaged seventy-eight miles a day, with leading winds for about half the time.

The southern route takes advantage of the steady, favourable trade winds, but is about five thousand miles long. The second *Mayflower* sailed this way in fifty-one days, but she had to average a hundred and five miles a day to cover the greater distance.

The great circle route will always be linked with the name of Cdr. R. D. Graham. To him belongs the honour due to a pioneer. For he had the imagination and courage to sail westward directly against the expected westerly winds. His initiative was rewarded by fair winds. In May 1934 he sailed his 7-ton gaff cutter *Emanuel*, alone, one thousand, seven hundred and sixty-five miles from Bantry in Southern Ireland to St. John's, Newfoundland. Winds were easterly. There were three heavy gales and he saw one iceberg. He averaged seventy miles a day without self-steering gear, an epic performance.

In August 1956 Lt.-Cdr. Hamilton became the second man to sail the great circle route to the New World single-handed. He went still further north in *Salmo*, sister-ship to *Vertue XXXV* and *Cardinal Vertue*. From Glasgow his course curved up to 58° N before slanting south again to Belle Isle Strait. He, too, averaged seventy miles a day also without a wind-vane. For seventeen of the twenty-nine days of his crossing he had to sail close-hauled. He encountered five gales and fog near Newfoundland, which lifted after ten days to reveal a large iceberg.

Cdr. Graham's *Rough Passage*, the deceptively modest article which Peter Hamilton contributed to *The Yachtsman*, and Humphrey Barton's book *Vertue XXXV*, were invaluable to us. Above all we are indebted to Graham, whose initiative led him to become one of the few in each age who have added to the stature of mankind by ripping strips off the tattered concept of impossibility.

There is an earlier sea rover, too, whose name should not be forgotten. Towards the close of the 10th century, one Biarne Hejrulfson was sailing from Iceland towards Greenland when "A north wind with fog set in and they knew not where they were sailing to, and this lasted many days. . . . At last they saw the sun and could distinguish the quarters of the sky. So they hoisted sail again and sailed a whole night and a day when they saw land."

As they were looking for Greenland, "with its great snow mountains", this tree-lined shore, probably Newfoundland, held no interest for the first Europeans to sight the Americas. So: "They left the land on the larboard side and had the sheet on the land side". But the gale increased and Biarne ordered a reef to be taken in and not to sail harder than the ship and her tackle could easily bear".

Eventually they reached Greenland, whence Leif Erikson and Thorfinn Karlsefri made a number of voyages of discovery to America as a result of Biarne's report.

It was another four hundred years before the Viking Greenlanders themselves faded from the pages of history and legend. A 14th-century seafarer gives a clue to how the climate had changed when he reports that: "It is only at peril of his life from ice that a man now sails the old route westward from Iceland to Greenland."

So the grey seas thunder unheeding at their passing, but their story is immortal.

On June 28th I was sitting in the dusk listening to the wind dying away and willing with all my soul that there would not be another calm. Then, suddenly, we emerged from under a great black arch of cloud to sail on under a clear pale greenish sky towards a crescent moon poised dramatically ahead. The gentle wind held, driving *Cardinal Vertue* on through the night.

I had fiddled with the tape-recorder until, to my surprise, it began to work. But now the radio had gone dead. I removed the back and stared in gloomy fascination at the incomprehensible maze of wires inside. I gingerly poked and prodded here and there until the valves suddenly glowed and a healthy sound of static crackled through the cabin. I hoped it would keep going but resolved to pay special attention to winding the deck-watch regularly. In any case no radio time signals were audible here, half-way between the continents, but I hoped to be able to obtain them later to correct the deck-watch and also to use the radio direction-finder to obtain bearings of coastal stations when feeling my way through the fog banks off the Canadian coast.

At dawn on June 29th, I hoisted the spinnaker. By noon we had made three consecutive daily runs of over a hundred miles. More than a thousand miles lay astern now. The keel was passing over a submarine mountain range which rises one and a half miles above the ocean floor. I passed a piece of driftwood around which a six-foot shark was lazily circling.

In the afternoon, because it was warm and sunny and the speed had dropped to half a knot, and the water was relatively shallow—only half a mile deep—I decided to have a swim. Tying a line round my waist, I plunged in. The water was cool but exhilarating, and I saw no weed on the ship's bottom. I was swimming about happily, luxuriating in the coolness flowing over my limbs and admiring my vessel, when I recalled the shark I had seen that morning, and a phrase from the Naval Life Saving Committee's shark papers came unbidden to mind.

"They . . . like to pluck legs which hang down from the surface like bunches of bananas. . . ."

An all too apt description that made me climb hurriedly aboard.

I celebrated the record runs with a large cooked meal of dehydrated chips, cold meat, dehydrated vegetables and stewed fruit. After such progress I decided that I could afford to use two matches a day now.

Over the undulating swells a steamer appeared. When she saw me she altered course abruptly to circle the yacht at slow speed. With clothes pegs I attached a notice written on the back of a chart to the dodger *"Single-handed Transatlantic Race. Please report to Lloyds,"* it read, my boat's name being already painted on the dodger. The officers waved from the bridge before the ship turned back to her course.

"Glad my friends will have news now," I wrote in the log. But *Sunetna* of Palermo did not report me.

For the next day, June 30th, this gloomy entry appears in the log: "Another calm, I can't describe the frustration. Unfortunately, I brought too little fat to cook the dehydrated chips—Never mind. . . . The sights are disappointing, the North Atlantic Drift is holding us back."

Soon a westerly wind set in, increasing in strength. The ever-recurring problem arose. Was it time to reduce sail? After I had lowered the genoa I commented in the log: "I thought so! I was overcautious. . . . The effect of that broken mast. . . . I have lost confidence when pounding to windward. . . . I cannot bear the thought of the dreary trail home with half a stick!"

Another depression was passing north of me; I accordingly came about to the starboard tack in expectation of the wind veering from south-of-west to north-west when the cold front passed. My proper course lay just south-of-west but I could afford to go further south still to miss being caught in an offshoot of the Labrador current which recurved eastward. By such tactics as these I hoped to make the best use of the contrary winds to bring me over the detached submarine plateau, Flemish Cap, and towards Cape Race beyond.

It was hard to make much progress that afternoon against the short steep seas, reminiscent of the Thames Estuary. But in compensation, a school of porpoises puffed and blew as they played alongside. Then, after dark, came one of the ocean's breathtaking moments. I was adjusting the self-steering gear when I glanced down to see the rudder swirling with cold phosphorescent fire and the log line trailing astern like a rapier sheathed in flame.

But in a few hours I was cursing the calm again, and casting a jaundiced eye at the yellow sunrise beneath the edge of the overcast. Gloomily I cooked breakfast; then hurriedly dropped everything to adjust sheets and wind-vane as a breeze from the north stirred the sails.

4

PALE SUNS AND STRAY BERGS

"What is a woman that you forsake her,
And the hearth-fire and the home-acre,
To go with the old grey Widow-maker?

She has no house to lay a guest in—
But one chill bed for all to rest in,
That the pale suns and the stray bergs nest in."
—RUDYARD KIPLING'S *Harp Song of The Dane Women.*

JULY 4th marked the end of my third week at sea. I was terrified of calms now, for out of those twenty-one days there had been fourteen with them. But all that day the wind held, so that the next morning I could write:

"This is what I came for! A squall came suddenly out of the north —the glass had been falling. I dropped the spinnaker smartly and hauled it from the sea, streaming phosphorescence. Soaked through by the driving wet mist, I renewed the tack lashing on the mainsail, then rolled down a third of the sail. After an hour everything had been adjusted, and as *Cardinal Vertue*, no longer overpressed, raced away westward, the stars suddenly broke out overhead, while Venus left a brilliant track over the waves. A glorious night with the spray frothing high! I am celebrating by using an extra match to light the cabin lamp and make coffee."

For thirty-six hours the alternating calms and depressions had not allowed me to sleep. Now I slept soundly until at 4 a.m. I was awakened by the ship wallowing, taken aback by the wind which had fallen light. With chilled fingers I unreefed and set her on course again; the cabin lamp glowed warmly and soon I was nursing a mug of hot soup while a pot of stew was heating on the stove.

I was wearing two pairs of socks, pyjamas underneath corduroys, a string vest, two Norwegian pullovers and a ski-ing anorak now, for the weather was colder as we neared the chilly Labrador current which flows south between Baffin Land and Greenland and then washes the shores of Labrador, Newfoundland, Nova Scotia and the New England States. I would enter the main stream of this current at the edge of the Grand Banks, from where it would help carry me southward.

Meanwhile I was still sailing through the eddies of the North Atlantic Drift, an extension of the Gulf Stream. At the junction of the two currents the sea temperature may change as much as 15°F in a ship's length. This meeting place is called the Cold Wall and here sediment and plankton are deposited.

For untold ages the cod have arrived each spring to feed, and every season for four hundred years fishermen have come to the Grand Banks for them. Many sealers and fishermen sleep here forever, for the icebergs from Davis Strait keep an unholy rendezvous with the rolling fog-banks which form where the currents mingle.

Another depression passed by, building the waves that similar winds might have produced in the English Channel. These steep seas would often stop *Cardinal Vertue* dead in her tracks.

It was becoming easier to tell when to reef. The ship would begin to pound; she would feel heavy and pressed down; sometimes she would luff into the gusts, so that the sails flogged and vibrated, making the whole ship shudder. Then, as the wind increased, she would be pressed down until the lee rail was forced under, and the speed dropped sharply.

I could decide better from down below whether the ship was over-pressed or lifting easier, for my judgment was not obscured by the noise of the wind, the spray and breaking crests and the size of the waves and the greyness of the surrounding murk.

The proper time to make and hand sail is a problem forever demanding accurate decision from a small boat sailor if he is to obtain maximum speed without endangering ship or gear. During the race I made eighty-seven major changes of headsails, reefed or unreefed the mainsail eighty-six times and hoisted the unwieldy spinnaker on ten occasions.

I had now reached the region of grey sea and grey skies; sunbathing was at an end. I did not remove my clothes again, unless I had been soaked, for a thousand miles.

For the first time the brown gulls, which often followed me, were joined by delicate black birds with a white stripe across their forked tails. They danced over the waves, flicking the water with beak or claw, daintily as kittens. I never saw one alight and these stormy petrels appeared too fragile to live on the face of the ocean.

Cooking had now become a matter of strict routine, but was still fun while some variety of food existed. Everything had to be planned and prepared beforehand, spoons, saucepan, kettle, food, all laid out in a row on the lee cabin side. The rest was a question of balance and anticipation of the ship's next movement. But it was pleasant cooking below at night while *Cardinal Vertue* lifted easily to the seas; the howling wind and the damp mist and spray driving past outside the doghouse windows made the cabin seem a more comfortable refuge.

Orderliness, routine and foresight in little things. There was something feminine about the meticulousness required in matters of detail, feminine too, many of the jobs that had to be done—mending clothes and sails, cleaning, cooking, washing. Too many men who pride themselves on their manliness, and regard "women's work" as beneath their male dignity, manifest their masculinity only in a bedroom; or more often in a bar, describing their exploits. Seamen and small boat sailors, soldiers on active service, explorers, mountaineers—all these spend much of their time, and indeed take pride in their mastery of "women's work".

I have often been asked how the ship remained on her course while I was asleep. The wind-vane kept her sailing at a constant angle to the wind, but what if the wind's direction changed? When this happened the rhythm of her motion across the waves altered. The new "feel" of the yacht, or her pounding when pressed too hard, or the judder of a vibrating sail, would be enough to wake me. In choppy weather I would be lying dressed in oilskins, rubber boots and, of course, the safety-belt. But this was to be avoided when possible as I awoke moist and clammy. The sleeping clothes I preferred in this weather included an anorak and rubber shoes.

So I crawled on westward. Calms alternated with contrary winds. I made desperately little progress.

There was always plenty of ship work to be done—carpentry, care of tools, oiling the log and steering vane, letters to write ready for posting ashore, lists to prepare of jobs to be done in New York in preparation for the return voyage, checking over the rigging, pumping and navigation. Often I had not the heart to tackle them.

Once I wrote "The hours do drag so! The Atlantic is so large! Six weeks is so long. The winds are so bloody unco-operative!" Sometimes I felt sorry for myself when the wind fell away and the spiky wavelets began to plop. "Grey overcast, grey sea! if only I had some butter, how much less like sawdust the biscuits would taste!" But soon my mood would lighten again as I read or preferably did something useful.

On July 8th I could look back on five days of hard struggle to win westing. For four of these days I had sailed on the port tack. At first during the night of July 4th-5th, I could lay my own course, but had to reef and unreef several times as the hours crawled on. No sleep, and next morning, hours of calm. Then another night of reefing, all in grey mist and fine driving rain.

On the 6th, heavy damp fog lay until evening, a day of calms, rain squalls, headwinds and short, vicious seas. When *Cardinal Vertue* plunged her bow into a wave the speed indicator needle would drop from three to three-quarters of a knot; she would shudder, fall away to leeward, then slowly gather way, only to be brought up short again.

Later, when I was hauling the mainsheet hard in, the clew fitting at the end of the boom, to which the sheet is attached, pulled right out. I could barely hold the boom and wriggled down to the wet cockpit floor to prevent it pulling me overboard. Then I clipped my safety-belt to a guard rail, slipped a bight of the mainsheet over the end of the boom and made it fast. It was secure for the moment. As I could not think what to do next, I went below and made tea.

The boom had been shortened before the trip so the deck blocks, through which the mainsheet was threaded, were now too far aft, with the result that the sheet tended to pull the fitting from the end of the boom.

I screwed eyes into the deck further forward, to which I shackled the blocks. Then I spread the clew fitting with Bostik, hammered it back, re-rove the sheet and hoped for the best. The job would have to be completed by fitting a new mainsheet horse in New York.

Cardinal Vertue, headed off course, continued to pound into the seas, sending up clouds of spray, through cold grey white-capped waves beneath a lowering overcast sky. I did not need to reef again until I was cooking dehydrated chips with nearly the last of the butter. The exasperated comment appears in the log that "the wind *always* comes up at the most awkward times. I have little fat of any sort, or milk, or sugar, but am catching up with the matches and can use three a day. It really is essential to make out a food list before starting a jaunt like this."

At 9 p.m. I was trying to light the cabin lamp from the stove, the ship doing her best to stand on end, when a deep "toot, toot" sounded outside. The sound did not register at first, but when it was repeated I dropped the frying pan and sprang up into the cockpit to see *White*

Rose of Helsingfors slowly circling me. I hung out my notice and the great ship came up to leeward going dead slow. A large vessel must keep downwind of a small sailing boat or she will blanket her wind and drift down upon her as she wallows helplessly. This captain was a real seaman who handled his giant as if she had been a launch. When he had read my message he hooted once again then, with passengers and crew waving good-bye, he turned away to the eastward, moving slowly at first so that the wake of his churning propellers should not harm me. I did not know it then, but this was the first time I was reported.

For four days I had been driven north of the proper track. On July 9th I was still unable to lay my course, but this time I was being forced to the south of it, punching head seas which made everything aboard shake and rattle. "On this starboard tack half the damned Atlantic comes into the ship," I wrote. "I think a seam must have opened. I had better fix the leak in New York or some bloody great shark will swim into the bilge. I keep note of the number of strokes with the pump that are needed—forty every few hours now. Still, with the diaphragm pump this is no hardship." This pump had been fitted beneath the cabin sole to supplement the standard one in the cockpit.

Beside the cross on the chart marking the noon position for July 9th is scrawled an unseamanlike, "Oh Mother!" for I had crossed a dotted line marking the mean maximum iceberg limit for July (U.S. Pilot Chart).

"God, it is so cold!" the log-book reads. "This north-west wind is blowing straight off the Barren Lands round Hudson Bay. The thermometer in the cabin reads 57°, but my toes tell me it is far colder. I only wish I could be extravagant with matches now for a hot drink would be welcome. Never mind; soon it will be evening, then a *very* large stew and lots of coffee. I wonder how the others are doing? No one could be as slow as me, not nearly: never, at my most pessimistic had I expected such poor progress as this. In the last twenty-four hours, one of the hardest days of beating to windward I have ever known, we gained eighteen miles! But I *will* get there."

July 13th was eventful. For the first time in ten days the wind was favourable. I was becoming accustomed to the spinnaker, which I was now able to set in half an hour as the vane steered *Cardinal Vertue* down wind. When the wind drew ahead a few hours later, and I had to change it for the genoa, we could still remain on course. I kept the genoa permanently hanked to the forestay when it was lowered, instead of spending time stowing it below, where it could not have dried any-way.

Gowens had made me a new mainsail, and twin staysails of heavy Terylene, before the race; but I had been unable to afford a new genoa as well. After all, working sails had to come before light weather ones. Accordingly I had written to Vertue owners whose addresses appeared in Lloyd's Register, asking for the loan of old genoas. Now, as well as my own elderly sail, genoas from the Vertues *Huzzar* and *Sally II* were aboard, so that I had something in hand when one tore. I had no wish to be like Alain Gerbault who had literally stitched his way across the Atlantic.

When I hoisted the genoa I would let the staysail stand, too, as the two sails did not appear to interfere with each other. The routine of lowering a headsail, as the wind gusted up, was well established. Leaving the sheet taut to stop the sail flogging, I would let go the halyard and allow the sail to drop into the water where it could come to no harm. Then I would lash the head to the pulpit, slacken the sheet, pull the rest aboard and make all fast. No strain on the sail, because it was not allowed to flap, quick, and no deviation from course.

At 5 p.m. fog closed down, thick and impenetrable.

Half an hour later I heard the first foghorn. As I was nearing the Grand Banks and the main Atlantic shipping lanes, I hoisted the radar reflector.

Twenty minutes later I heard the beat of a ship's engine and hurried on deck. A towering shape was looming out of the fog to port, two cables off, moving dead slow. I could hear the crew talking and dis-tinguish their words. There was a moment of panic until I saw that the steamer was passing clear. She disappeared into the fog up wind, her engines remaining audible for a full twenty minutes.

Before the sound had faded, other engines were thumping and foghorns sounding in various keys. A bell was being rung every four minutes from one vessel. On another metal was being struck. These must be fishing-boats at anchor. The one place where they could reach bottom was Flemish Cap, the submerged plateau that rises from the abyss to within twenty-eight fathoms of the surface, and lies three hundred and forty miles east of Cape Race, Newfoundland. It is a rich fishing ground. Here was I, in fog, threading through an invisible fishing fleet and crossing a main Atlantic shipping lane into the bargain! I wished that the fog would lift so that I could see the boats and talk to their crews, but it remained as thick as ever.

Once a siren began to blare very loudly, engines throbbed and a halo of light appeared through the mist. Then it slid by.

For two hours I was becalmed, but by 11 p.m. the genoa was drawing well and the sound of foghorns was growing fainter astern. A long musical note rang out from the topmast stay each time *Cardinal Vertue* curtsied to a swell. She was singing to herself as she climbed the slope of the Continental Shelf which was rising from a depth of two miles, a few days' sail astern, to the hundred-fathom line about forty miles ahead.

At midnight on July 13th it was 10 p.m.! This is no slip of the pen. I had put my watch back two hours—the wrist-watch, that is. The deck-watch or chronometer was always kept at Greenwich Mean Time. So far I had also used G.M.T. for my daily routine, but with every 15 degrees of westing, the sun rose and set an hour later. By now sunset was well after midnight and dawn 9 a.m.! So, as I was nearing land, I decided to fall in line with those on shore.

Another half an hour back would put the clock to Newfoundland Summer Time. Nova Scotian time is four hours behind Greenwich; New York (Eastern Standard Time) is five hours slow. I would now have to note my G.M.T. noon position in the log at 10 a.m. by my wrist-watch. Off New York, G.M.T. noon would be at 7 a.m. E.S.T.!

In keeping with the mood of these two nameless hours a sense of unreality possessed me. With the gentle breeze from the north-west *Cardinal Vertue* tended to fall away to port towards the distant sound of the foghorns, so I dare not relax too much.

The log reads "I am very tired. For more than a week now I have slept only in short snatches dictated by the veering and backing of the winds. I must keep awake in case we sag down wind into that traffic jam. But now we are clear of the actual shipping the tiredness is creeping back. There is a slight ringing and the sound of voices in my ears and the familiar feeling that I am not alone."

The relative lack of hallucinations on this voyage had been a surprise. When I was very tired, and had spent monotonous hours at the helm in winds too light for the vane, I sometimes heard voices. For one whole day in fog the sea appeared to slope up-hill; during a foggy night I had seemed to be sailing on a height with the lights of two passing steamers on a plain far below. But these occasions were rare.

It had been very different the previous summer when I had sailed alone to Norway and back without a wind-vane. Then, after several days at sea, particularly when very tired in the hours before dawn, there came a distinct feeling of having been divided into two personalities, one of which would speak to the other, and sometimes would advise. At times it appeared that another person was at the helm, while the other "part personality" was critically observing his actions and problems.

Slocum describes such an incident during bad weather in mid-Atlantic, when another entity appeared to take charge. He was a good storyteller and with true dramatic instinct identified his "guest" as the pilot of Columbus' ship *Pinta*.

However, one episode of de-personalization occurred during my return from Norway, different from those usually described. A block and tackle gadget, which I had myself rigged up at sea to help me alter course without leaving the cabin, became consistently identified in my mind as of feminine construction.

"While fully aware that he had rigged it up himself," I wrote later; "the subject was never able to accept it as his own work but always distrusted this product of 'feminine' ingenuity, and when it went wrong cursed himself heartily for allowing a 'woman' to meddle with his ship. This attitude persisted throughout the three days during which the arrangement was in use. Is it too fanciful to regard this as a de-personalization in which the feminine-like component of the subject's character stood apart?"

I had seen imaginary rivers flowing through green, bush-clad valleys in New Zealand when, as a boy of seventeen, I paddled a home-made canoe some four hundred and thirty miles along rivers, lakes and estuaries, from my school in Wanganui to my home in Auckland. Solitude, exhaustion and monotony seem to be the common factors underlying these experiences. Blondie Hasler's war-time hallucinations in two-seater canoes during the training period for his "Cockle-shell" raid on Bordeaux tend to bear this out, for the two men, sitting one behind the other, were virtually isolated. After five or six hours' paddling at night phantom ships or buoys would appear. Once Blondie became so annoyed on finding his companion "reading *The Times*", that he was about to remonstrate forcibly when he realized they were creeping through a pitch-dark night without lights! During the actual operation, however, no such phenomena occurred.

I am interested in the effects of solitude and fatigue, because they may throw light on something far more fundamental—the deep-seated urge that drives modern civilized man to seek adventure in the remote places of the earth. I think this has always been part of the essential dynamic nature of the human spirit, but in early ages it found a ready outlet in the individual combat of battle and raiding, in piracy, and along the equally perilous pathways of legitimate trade.

Since about the middle of the 19th century, wars have become increasingly mechanized, impersonal and inhumanly destructive, while the industrial revolution brought relative security, scientific advance and a vast, flat drabness. You could no longer starve or die of plague in civilized countries, but neither could you seek new worlds beyond the sunset. Instead, you might compete with the Jones's in the dullness of your life and the uselessness of your possessions.

Surely it is no accident that this was the period when men began to climb mountains without carrying thermometers, or collecting urine samples for analysis? Nor did they climb for the view, but simply because the mountain was there. The wakes of small boats were soon criss-crossing every ocean. Men like Slocum and Voss did not sail around the world for gold or empire, but simply to fulfil something within themselves. True, Alain Bombard sacrificed his health and risked his life in an attempt to prove his theory and save others, but a less adventurous man would have devised experiments that were not so rigorous (and, incidentally, more effective in finding the answers to still unsolved problems). Adventurous undertakings, not foolhardy ones, have become accepted.

Hasler thinks that people should take controlled risks from time to time to keep themselves up to scratch and be in the best possible physical, mental and emotional condition to react to any sudden emergency. My own experiences as a doctor have convinced me that fully a third of illnesses arise directly from a chronic state of anxiety and lack of courage and self-confidence. Increased social security has not abolished this dread of nameless disaster. Uncertainty, fears and a want of self-respect are rife. Those who have known physical fear, but have learned to control it, seem less prone to these disorders. Of course, security is necessary but security is only one aspect of life— man must also have things to fight and strive for, and so enhance the dignity of his life.

This, I think, was the real reason why we were making this trip. Different as were our natures, attitudes to life, to the sea or to the race, we were driven by much the same force. For each one of us, the problems of getting away, of expense, of learning the skill required, had appeared insuperable, yet something within us had refused to acknowledge the limits of the practical and the possible.

I do not think the concept of escapism applies to undertakings that require so much positive planning and effort. It is true we may simply have been abnormal people, but the encouraging support given to us before the race, and the way in which the idea captured public imagination, revealed that innumerable men and women shared the same feelings and urges and, but for economic and domestic reasons, might themselves have taken part.

It has been argued that endeavour and adventure are of no practical value. But is it more useful to devote one's life to earning money, only to end it by a coronary thrombosis brought on by the effort and worry? I do not know.

Another misconception is that adventurers seek risks. Although there may well be an element of danger in anything worth while, the challenge is in using one's judgment, knowledge and skill to avoid trouble. Two of the finest small boat sailors today are Eric and Susan Hiscock. They know so much—and plan so well—that they have sailed round the world without any serious mishaps. It is those less skilled whose adventures may become rather too exciting for comfort —as I was soon to find out.

Something of the spirit of our race can be caught by the wording of one of the rules. "Yachts must be fully independent and capable of carrying out their own emergency repairs at sea. Crews have no right to expect or demand rescue operations to be launched on their behalf."

In its whole conception the race was supremely an adventure and a challenge. But unlike other single-handed voyages it provided a special opportunity to study the reactions of several men who would each be isolated in similar conditions and perhaps be exposed to fear and hardship. In other words the situation had the makings of a controlled experiment.

I wrote to medical and scientific authorities in England and as far afield as the U.S.A. and Italy. What useful data could the race yield? How best to obtain it?

Eventually I was introduced to Dr. Harold Lewis of the Medical Research Council. He is a quiet South African who had directed the medical research when he was on the British North Greenland Expedition of 1952–1954. There was nothing unusual about his office at the Division of Human Physiology in Hampstead except for files bearing such labels as "Sledging Rations—Antarctic", "Sleep Rhythms

—Greenland", "Fat Thickness—Polar Expeditions". He was now helping to build up a school of Polar physiology, and was interested in all techniques involving field-work. He readily consented to co-operate, for here was a unique opportunity to learn about the eating and sleeping habits, the mental and physical feelings of men in isolation. This sort of information, though very valuable, is usually almost impossible to obtain, and would be particularly applicable in solving problems of survival at sea.

With the blessing of the Medical Research Council we soon had the necessary advisers in psychology, nutrition and statistics. We worked out a plan whereby I (with Hasler and Howells who both agreed to help) would be the advance party in the field, with the team of experts as the base laboratory. It was a pretty wide base because Harold had contacted experts in England and in New York!

Broadly speaking, we were going to study daily changes of mood, the sleep rhythm, food and water intake, using a daily questionnaire. We wanted notes to be made promptly and so we produced for the race competitors a "Medical Log-book", extracts from which are reproduced in Appendix Four.

It was not easy to fill in this medical log regularly when one felt sick or tired, or just bemused by being violently shaken in a boat that lurched and bucked ceaselessly. Yet Howells and Hasler, in spite of their other pressing tasks, spent an hour each day conscientiously completing the record.

My own feelings are pungently expressed in a tape-recording made during our second week at sea:

"This 'brilliant' product of the fervent imaginations of H. L. and myself! How beautifully printed by the M.R.C. and how often I have cursed it these last few days! But it will be really valuable to have a daily record of our feelings because memory of emotions so quickly fades and disappears into the background. I cannot recall accurately my own feelings of a few days ago now. Some memories do remain—How it felt to sail blindly through fog for those four nights—or the other night when I had boomed out the staysails. Damp mist dripped everywhere, the foredeck looked like a battlefield of tangled ropes; a foghorn was hooting somewhere abeam. Then, the moment the sails were drawing, the ship ceased to roll and glided away smoothly through

---

7. (*Opposite*) Blondie Hasler's *Jester* with *Cardinal Vertue* in light airs in the Solent.

8. Race preparations at Plymouth. *Gipsy Moth III* is in the foreground and, facing her from left to right, *Eira*, *Jester* and *Cardinal Vertue*.

the mist and darkness. That moment, and others like it, will remain with me always."

This is a long digression from my efforts to keep awake. It was not until 2.30 a.m. next morning, July 14th, after the wind had completely boxed the compass and was again blowing from the south-west, that I could come on to the port tack and head away from the faint sound of foghorns. I turned in wearing full equipment but had only an hour's sleep before the genoa had to come in. Ninety minutes later the main-sail needed reefing and in another hour it had to be close-reefed, and the staysail reefed as well. I was becoming more proficient, so that close-reefing the main and staysail now took only seventeen minutes.

At dawn, the sea was wild and beautiful. Crests burst over the ship with surprising violence as she plugged to windward against a force 6 breeze. Sometimes the impact of a breaking sea would bring her up all standing.

I dared not relax with wind and seas increasing, so to stave off my desperate need for sleep I forced myself to cook and eat a little, then washed up, no mean feat with the yacht's wild motion. Encouraged by this success and being unable to stand the reflection in the mirror opposite the companionway, I shaved. Then it was time to plot my estimated G.M.T. noon position, 47° N 47° W—an encouraging day's run of seventy-five miles. But soon the wind dropped completely and we lay becalmed for eight and a half hours.

That evening the fog lifted briefly in a squall of icy rain. The air temperature was 50° as *Cardinal Vertue* entered the zone where fog lies for 40 per cent. of the time in July. We were also crossing "Iceberg track C" (*Newfoundland and Labrador Pilot*), which runs south at the eastern edge of the Grand Banks and is the most usual route along which the bergs drift.

Every time I looked out of the cabin breaking phosphorescent crests momentarily set my nerves on edge. There had not been a satisfactory longitude sight for the past two weeks and for the first time in filling in the medical log I placed a cross in the column "Wish it were all over".

In view of the conditions I judged it appropriate to broach the "Survival Kit only effective west of 35° W", which I had been given at Plymouth and which so far had served as a successful "iceberg repellent" when taken at bedtime—a new use for gin!

Another day and a seemingly interminable night wore on. If my dead reckoning was correct, I should be crossing the edge of the Grand Banks into soundings early in the morning.

It was 4 a.m. on July 16th when I switched on the echo-sounder—it read forty fathoms! Two thousand miles of open Atlantic now lay astern.

As the light grew it showed a sea no longer indigo blue, but a vivid bottle green. Air temperature was 53°, sea temperature 50°. We had crossed the Cold Wall into the south-flowing Labrador current and were over the Grand Banks.

The sea was already flecked with white. The waves increased and grew steeper, until by 7 a.m. the wind was whining out of the east at forty-one miles an hour (force 8) while from a lowering grey sky sheets of rain swept down, penetrating every nook and cranny in the cabin. But what of that! It was a wild and beautiful sight as *Cardinal Vertue* ran before the gale under her boomed staysail.

By midnight the wind had fallen enough to allow me to hoist the mainsail. In the enormous sea that was still running this took an hour. However, wasted time worried me less than the alarming discovery that the gooseneck of the boom, where it pivots against the mast, was badly bent. The boom could still be rotated however, so that roller reefing was still possible.

In the early hours of the morning the topping-lift parted and wound itself perversely round the cross-trees; then the radar reflector sustained damage. Repairs were completed before dawn and then I set out to hoist the spinnaker and free the self-steering gear, which was sticking; tasks occupying another one and a half hours.

The wind died down as the day advanced, until the ballooning blue spinnaker which had been drawing us proudly over the swells began to crinkle, then wound itself firmly about the topmast stay. I tried to clear it but the delicate nylon fabric was foul of the very top of the stay, 34 feet above the deck. Knowing that the longer I put off the inevitable the more frightened I would become, I stripped off my boots and jerseys and went up, over the lower cross-trees, up again until my feet rested on the upper pair, and then on further to the masthead. How that mast swept to and fro across the sky as *Cardinal Vertue* rolled to the oily swells passing under her! As soon as the sail was cleared I slid to the deck to find my legs trembling and my hands shaking with exertion and reaction from fear.

Soon, even the light breeze died away. I was cheered a little to see a whale break surface to port and blow, but it dived again immediately and did not reappear. Then a puffin, a comical little bird with a huge hooked nose and short wings that whirred up and down, came buzzing busily around the yacht, looking for all the world like the animated hub of an aircraft propeller.

That night I made a little progress but was again becalmed next morning. The fifth week had ended. The engine was useless; only three hundred and sixty miles of westing in the last seven days; but on six of them there had been calms and for six days fog.

Cape Race radio beacon was sounding loud and clear about fifty miles to the north-westward. I was nearing Newfoundland, but that day, though I knew nothing of it at the time, Francis Chichester was closing the U.S.A., while Blondie Hasler was approaching Sable Island, off the coast of Nova Scotia.

Blondie's great sweep into the north had helped him little. South of Ireland on June 17th, when he had been six days at sea and I four, he was a little over two hundred miles ahead. When he had regained the direct route a little east of Flemish Cap on July 7th, he was approximately two hundred and sixty miles in front of me. Since then, outside of the worst belt of calms, he had widened the gap.

There was not a ship to be seen; neither fishing smack, nor trawler, nor dory. The Grand Banks seemed deserted as I floated in an uneasy quiet. There was nothing but grey sky and sea and the ghosts of *Bluenose* and the great Grand Banks schooners of yesterday.

But I did not feel lonely, for the old ships which had fished those waters for four hundred years seemed to bear me company, while the wraiths of the dragon ships of Lief and Thorvald and Karlsefni came stealing out of the northern mists across nine centuries.

5

THE THUNDERING SURF

"It is not advisable to approach the coast within the 40-fathom line; it must be borne in mind that this depth may be found within a distance of three miles of some of the most formidable dangers on the coast."

—Nova Scotia and Bay of Fundy Pilot
(Tenth Edition, 1958, page 85).

ON July 19th the log recorded that Cape Race radio beacon still bore a little west of north, much the same as it had two days before; these had been largely days of calm.

Sometimes the speed indicator would begin to register: half a knot, then *Cardinal Vertue* would be taken aback and I would spend a quarter of an hour gybing her back on course again. Usually the tiny breeze would be contrary. Next a puff might come from astern; up spinnaker! But in ten minutes the wind would be hushed again and the enormous ocean swell would be sending everything that was free to move crashing to and fro.

Compass variation had reached maximum and would begin to decrease from now on. At Plymouth the variation had been 10°W, that is, the magnetic compass needle pointed 10 degrees west of true north. As a ship sails westwards towards Newfoundland, the variation increases until it reaches 28 degrees off Cape Race; for the needle indicates the bearing of the Magnetic Pole, which is situated in northeast Canada. Off New York it has become 11 degrees again.

As charts are marked with lines of equal variation, there is no problem for the navigator if he remembers the sailor's rhyme: "Variation west, magnetic best." This means he must subtract variation from compass reading to obtain a true bearing.

Four days earlier, a check on the water showed that with my present rate of consumption and progress there would be barely enough to last to New York. The reasons for the shortage were: calms far in excess of those predicted by the pilot charts, and an underestimation of the amount of water needed to reconstitute the dehydrated food. As I had now eaten most of the things I liked best, there was little food left aboard except dehydrated. Furthermore, even worse calms were to be expected in July along the Atlantic sea-board of the United States.

I took the following steps: fresh water was rationed to one and a half pints a day for all purposes. In order to reduce my kidney output to a minimum, I went without any fluids whatever for the first twenty-four hours of rationing. This step is essential when fluid has to be conserved, as the slightly increased concentration of the blood which results automatically signals to the kidneys to "Shut down". The experience was less unpleasant than might have been supposed.

Rain water had to be collected. I emptied all large tins aboard and put them in the cockpit whenever it rained. This was often enough now; so that in the first twenty-four hours I caught four and a half pints, mostly in the canvas spray hood. Some samples were contaminated by spray, but even these could be used for cooking.

The dehydrated food presented the biggest problem. Most solid foods contain 60–80 per cent. water, which has to be added to reconstitute dehydrated food. Some salt water can be used for the meat and vegetables, but the highest ratio I could tolerate was one part of salt water to three of fresh. I tried more but it made me sick.

However, I found that if the tins or packets were opened, and their contents were exposed to the moist sea air in the cockpit for about twenty-four hours, they would absorb a good deal of moisture. For instance, the brittle dehydrated "plastic chips" which used to need ten ounces of fresh water, only required two ounces of fresh and two ounces of salt, after twelve hours "airing". I concluded the note in the log by writing: "In case this sounds alarming: (a) By the rules of the race, I *can* put into any port to stock up (St. John's is only a few days away). However, I have no intention of putting in and wasting any more time. (b) I am conserving supplies so strictly that I will soon have some in hand. (c) There are three solar stills aboard which can be blown up and used to convert salt water to fresh, but I am keeping them in reserve for use further south where the sun is stronger. Once in the water, the stills cannot be brought aboard again, and if towed at any speed will capsize and become contaminated. However, these gadgets are ideal for use with a rubber raft. (d) There is an extra two gallons of water in a plastic jerry-can attached to the emergency rubber raft."

Rubber rafts were the main items of the emergency equipment supplied to us through the Naval Life Saving Committee. They are normally blown up by CO_2 cylinders, but these did not turn up at Plymouth in time.

When these one-man rafts arrived, they had been piled on my deck. I passed one to each of the others and put another below for myself. There must have been several over, however, because when I had time to sort things out at sea, I found I had no less than three—a miniature armada, I thought, if ever I had to use them!

The rafts had complete covers, for the main cause of loss of life among castaways is cold, aggravated by dampness and wind which soon disperses body heat. So a "fug" must be produced in which heat loss is prevented.

The second enemy is thirst; a man may live fifty days without food but rarely as long as two weeks when deprived of water. About one and a half pints is the least daily requirement to maintain health but with four-fifths of a pint a person's condition will only deteriorate gradually, unless fluid loss is accelerated by a hot climate, seasickness or diarrhoea.

The highest concentration of salt with which the kidneys can deal is 0.8 per cent., but sea water contains 3.5 per cent. of salt. If it is drunk, the excess of salt must be excreted and dissolved in water derived from the body fluids, so that the result is likely to be a net loss of liquid. There is still argument as to whether small amounts of sea water are helpful, useless, or lethal, to castaways. Until more is known, it would be safer to abstain.

The plastic jerry-can of emergency fresh water was tied to a large kit-bag into which had been stuffed my survival gear. The water-can would float, as fresh water is lighter than salt. The remaining contents of the kit-bag, in addition to a rubber raft, were food, a solar still, fishing kit, the lifeboat chart of the North Atlantic, a protractor for gauging the approximate latitude, a compass and a heliograph mirror for signalling. Stored separately were distress rockets.

The food was entirely carbohydrate (sugars and starches), five ounces a day for two weeks. No protein was included because protein foods cause the body to lose water when their waste products are excreted. On the other hand a small portion of the carbohydrate consumed is broken down by the body into water.

"The glass is higher than ever now; will this calm never break?" I wrote on the 19th. "I am trying every plan. Going over the wind roses on the pilot charts, pilot books and tide-tables. Can I work the tides, drifting and anchoring along the coasts of Nova Scotia and Maine? Reluctantly I decide against it. The coastline is too broken and the sea too deep right up to the cliffs for anchoring; nor are the land and sea breezes helpful off Nova Scotia; but I could use the method off Long Island if necessary.

"Graham in *Emanuel* took twenty-five days from Bantry to St. John's. My thirty-two days from south of Mizzen Head (opposite Bantry) to Cape Race (near St. Johns) has been pretty bad. Hamilton sailed from Glasgow to Belle Isle in twenty-nine days. But—neither of these had calms!"

My calms up to noon on July 19th had totalled four days twenty-one hours! I learnt later that Blondie Hasler had made the passage from the entrance to Bantry Bay to off St. John's in some twenty-seven days.

"The problem of morale is all important. I can do nothing about the lack of wind, so let me see what I *can* do.

"Use every zephyr. This means little rest day or night and a lot of steering because the vane does not function under two and a half knots. See to everything that needs doing, e.g. oiling reefing gear—have to force myself out of apathy into activity—but feel the better for it! With the New England coast notorious for calms, I have to expect even more calms now, so must collect rain water. For the past three days have been using rain water only, so am doing quite well. Must avoid slackness, as last night when I kept on the less advantageous tack. The direction was all right but I neglected to look up the pilot chart during the night, so entered a contrary current. I will note down everything that will be needed in New York; replacements, repairs and food lists, *now*, so that I can start back with the least possible delay. And *what* a lot of water and butter and matches the ship will carry! She will be loaded down with books and magazines and have a spare battery, so there will be electric light!

"The last thing about morale is that underneath the bitterness at the calms, the frustration of knowing I have failed in the race, being sorry for myself, and suchlike stupid feelings, plus some real loneliness now, there is gradually emerging a quiet but very grim determination to get there. There seems to be an inner and quite unexpected strength of purpose. It is not melodrama but plain certainty to say that I am going to get to New York in this boat no matter how long it takes and even if I have to arrive there starving!"

Six hundred miles away Val Howells, too, was feeling depressed.

"Progress good, but morale terrible," he wrote that day. "Shedding tears over wife and family."

Blondie also had his troubles. "Over-ate last night," his medical log records!

The evening of July 19th brought wind. "Lord, I am tired!" I had written, after hours of attempting to use largely illusory breezes. But I was to have little sleep that night; just half-hourly snatches, interrupted by having to climb sleepily out onto the transom and squat down, swaying to the ship's rolling, poised over the boiling phosphorescence which swirled off the rudder, to adjust the self-steering gear which needed a lot of attention with a variable wind on the quarter. But the effort was worth while, for by noon G.M.T. next day, 9 a.m. ship's time, *Cardinal Vertue* had covered sixty miles since 9 p.m. the previous night, an average of exactly five knots.

She kept going all day in rain squalls, fog and gathering seas. First the genoa had to be handed, then the mainsail reefed. The glass had fallen to 1,008 mb from its reading of 1,025 mb during the last calm.

Twice the sun broke through the clouds, each time allowing me to obtain a sight. It was a luxury to be able to pin-point the day's position like this, and to have an additional guide in the soundings of the banks below!

During the evening of July 20th we sailed free of the iceberg zone that we had been crossing for eleven days.

"After all that nervous strain," I wrote, "not to have seen even one seems unfair."

I was disturbed that night by an irregular banging in the weather scuppers. Perhaps a halyard was flogging or a stay had parted? I hurried on deck to inspect the rigging with a torch, but nothing seemed out of place. Still the noise continued. Then I shone the torch downwards, to see a glistening blue-green fish, about 10 inches long, with all the glowing colour of the sea in him, flopping about on the deck where he had been cast by a breaking sea. There was a wild scramble before I grabbed him and dropped him down the companionway. I felt rather treacherous towards a fellow sea creature, but I was hungry enough to be ruthless.

Later that night the hourly soundings petered out as we left astern St. Pierre Bank, the westernmost of the Grand Banks, and headed out across the trench scoured by the waters of the St. Lawrence as they emerge from Cabot Strait. The wind now headed us so that we had to plug to windward, unable to lay course against force 4 and 5 breezes and short seas that threw the ship bodily sideways, and still further to leeward. In the open sea without landmarks it is difficult to judge how well a boat is sailing, but I estimated that in these conditions I could only make good sixty degrees from the wind.

"I just can't get used to the motion going hard to windward, especially when she is pressed a bit and leaping about, pounding, swept by spray and shuddering from time to time at the impact of a breaking sea," I wrote. "If the wind does drop a little, I often don't realize, in all the cuffufle of sea and violent motion, especially when I am over-tired and my judgment clouded and my mental processes slow, that it is time to unreef.

"As a result I am often too slow at making sail when the wind is dropping—of course one doesn't want to mistake a lull, after which the wind may blow harder than ever, for a real easing. Sometimes I go on deck two or three times with the mast winch handle, and hold my hand, and am glad to have done so.

"The strain on a ship's gear, other things being equal, is proportionate to her displacement. A heavy displacement boat like *Cardinal Vertue* sets up considerable stresses in her mast and rigging in a seaway. Therefore to some extent one has to reef in accordance with the violence of the sea as well as the strength of the wind. However, as I am of a timid disposition, I find that I tend to be too easily overawed by the size of the waves."

Following a new train of thought I continued: "I must say I would be glad to talk to people again. It is five and a half weeks since I spoke to a soul. It is not only people I miss but food and drink, too. That fresh fish for lunch has whetted my appetite; but I can't find the fish hooks!

"I wish the wind would change. It has been right on the nose for twenty-three hours now. But what can I do about it? Slocum thought praying for a favourable wind a waste of time. On the other hand the Vikings, even after their conversion, thought highly of the competence of 'Old Red Beard'—Thor—in dealing with such matters as winds, storms and fighting."

My wishes remained unfulfilled, for when the line squall awakened me at 5.30 a.m. on the 22nd and I clambered sleepily on deck, the wind had changed and a row of black clouds lay to leeward, but I still could not lay the course. Swearing feebly, I rolled down 3 feet of the main and came about. Everything got in the way, as it does when one is half asleep.

The glass rose, but the wind was not dropping and the ship was being pressed still harder. This problem of how much sail to carry was presented anew each day. It was the sea's challenge. I held up the windspeed indicator: thirty-four to thirty-seven miles per hour, force 7, and squally too! No wonder she was labouring!

So I rolled down more mainsail until 7½ feet of it had been wound round the boom. This is as much as it can be reefed and still leave enough to function as a sail.

The yacht would not tolerate the full No. 1 staysail and I was grateful for Humphrey Barton's advice to have reef points in this sail, for it is infinitely easier to reef it than to change to a smaller sail. I dropped the staysail into the sea and sat wedged on the plunging, reeling, foredeck with my safety-belt clipped to a stay, tying the reef points.

Once the sail had been hoisted and sheeted in, *Cardinal Vertue* porpoised to windward, thudding and jumping. The wind had not yet had time to raise a big sea, though long lines of foam were beginning to run from the frothing white crests. Now it was blowing at forty miles an hour, force 8. I had not believed it possible for a small yacht to beat to windward in the open sea in a gale, but I now saw that it was, provided the shape and steepness of the seas allowed.

It was a wonderful, bright morning. As the seas built higher, the self-steering vane would be almost becalmed in the troughs between the waves. We were working across the strait between Newfoundland and Nova Scotia. The wind eased towards evening, but rose later, so that I had to reef again at 2.30 a.m. and close reef at 5 a.m. when the yacht was pressed hard over.

I was sleepily beginning to stir when a violent crack sounded from above and a sail began to flog wildly. "My God, the gooseneck has gone!" I thought, as I struggled into my P.V.C. smock and boots. The pawl that engages the ratchet on the roller reefing gear had slipped, partly because the entire fitting had now become loose on the boom. I smeared it with Bostik and hammered it home. Then, with great care, I close-reefed the mainsail and reefed the staysail; while low, ragged clouds scudded by from the westward, beneath a high sheet of alto-cumulus, which was already becoming tinged by the dawn.

It was blowing force 7 on that lowering morning of the 23rd, as the ship crashed her way into soundings across Missaine Bank, the first of the Nova Scotian Banks, south of Cape Breton Island. We had been sailing hard to windward for the past seventy hours, during sixty-nine of which I had been unable to lay course. No sights had been possible for three days. During the night the sky had cleared enough to show stars, for only the fourth time since leaving England. The lights of several ships had passed as they steamed south out of the St. Lawrence. "Every ship passes at night or in fog. I would like the opportunity of being reported," I wrote sadly. The chance was to come only too quickly!

At 4.45 p.m. the silhouettes of four warships in line astern appeared through the murk. One changed course and came towards me, throwing aside sheets of spray as she ploughed through the head sea set up by the force 5–6 breeze.

The Canadian frigate *Swansea* swung round to port of me, on to my weather side, her crew lining the decks as she manœuvred. How excited I was to see so many people!

I told them who I was and asked them to report me to Lloyds. The conversation was direct; the captain using his loud-hailer and myself shouting. My words were relayed when necessary by the crew. The captain acknowledged my request to be reported.

"Do you want your position?" he enquired.

"No, thank you," I answered untruthfully, for I was too proud to admit before such an audience that I had no idea exactly where I was.

They called "Good luck" and started to go ahead; but for some reason slowed again and wallowed to a stop, dead to windward of me. The crew began taking photographs and called more questions; they did not seem to realize the danger in which they were placing me.

In a moment my close-reefed mainsail and reefed staysail were flapping idly, all wind blanketed by the steel monster bearing down upon me. I called desperately for them to go ahead; no one heeded. Then the grey steel hull crashed against my planking, stripping off paint each time we rolled and scraped together. I was sobbing with helpless anger and frustration as I made futile efforts to fend off with a boat-hook.

Much shouting now began from the deck above, where everyone seemed to be giving orders at once, with no visible effect. "Go ahead or to starboard, you idiots!" I yelled furiously.

Then at last they did do something. They went *astern*. As the frigate rasped her way past me the high flare of her bow caught in my rigging and tore the port lower spreader out of its socket, splitting the wood from the thin bolt which held it. Failure of the starboard lower spreader had caused the loss of my mast off Plymouth.

Frantically I lowered all sail and throwing off oilskins, boots and jersey, shinned up the wildly gyrating mast to inspect the damage. Thank God, the cross-tree itself was not broken! Down again to collect a hammer, knife and insulation tape and tie them to my wrist. Then up to the cross-trees again where I was able to get a leg over the starboard one and clipped on my safety-belt in case I should be flicked into the sea; for *Cardinal Vertue* was rolling so violently now that at the end of each dizzy swing I had not strength enough to hold on by myself.

I cut the lashing which attached the spreader to the shroud and hammered it straight and back into its socket. Then I bound the inner

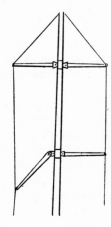

part with insulation tape; the outboard end would have to wait for calmer weather. I slid to the deck and clung to the mast, retching and trembling; wet through with sweat and soaked in spray; mouth open, gasping for breath as I rested my aching limbs.

A hail caused me to look over my shoulder. A pinnace circled near, from which the captain of *Swansea* apologized and asked if I needed help.

"Against the rules of the race, but thank you," I called. "Please report my position."

I hoisted sail at five-thirty. It seemed unbelievable that the whole incident had occupied only half an hour! The wind had dropped a little but we were sailing on the port tack so that the strain came on the damaged cross-tree.

"I only hope to God it holds," I wrote. "My fingers can hardly write from trembling, I am trying to keep dry and get warm, but my torn P.V.C. trousers have been inadequately mended.

"The frigate stood by until I was well under way, then with spray showering over her decks as she got up speed, she was soon swallowed by the mist." She never reported me. "Now the only thing to do is to hang on," I continued. "It is no good reducing sail 'in case'; if the mast is going it will go; I have to know its strength if it is going to last."

I was shivering with cold in my damp clothes and longing for coffee or a chance to crawl between blankets to rest my body which was aching and bruised from the buffeting received on the mast. But the wind had risen to force 7 again, and the ship was pounding and burying her lee rail. I close-reefed to ease her, then wrote doubtfully: "I *think* I reefed for the same wind force as I would have before the accident and was not influenced by my fear—that is something, anyway! I have to live with the damaged spreader, so had best come to terms with it right now!"

Now that there was time to make coffee, the Calor gas cooker jet had burned out. Over a tiny yellow flame I was eventually able to heat one mug of water. I was too tired to eat, even if I could have cooked anything.

I added a postscript to the day's log entry:

"Dead reckoning not going so well tonight. Soundings of banks won't square with my estimated position. Now I wish I hadn't been too proud to accept my position, when the frigate offered it—still, I would do exactly the same again!"

During the night the wind was variable, so that sheets and steering needed frequent adjustment. I awoke after an hour's sleep at 5 a.m. on July 24th, feeling very tired and most reluctant to crawl on deck into a damp fog. I had unreefed the staysail and was trying to decide whether the dying wind and slopping sea justified more mainsail, when a squall screamed out of the mist to windward and heeled the yacht over until she raced along crashing into the seas, with water cascading over her lee deck.

The clew fitting began to slip out again, so feeling depressed, I hammered it home. The stove would not burn, the leach of the mainsail was vibrating where a batten had been lost, the weakened spreader was putting the mast in danger—things seem to be getting on top of me!

"I cut down and shaped a spare batten, only to find that I could not reach to fit it into its pocket without lowering the sail." I noted, then added: "But heave-to unnecessarily in a race such as this I will not do, so am carrying on with the sail vibrating!"

By 6.30 a.m. I had turned my attention to the stove and had it partly dismantled when the squall increased. As I rolled down more mainsail, I found that the bent gooseneck fitting was slipping again. "Nothing I can do about it," I wrote, "Except slacken the sheet for the shortest possible time when reefing or unreefing, because while the sheet remains taut, the boom is held in firmly against the mast."

Back to the stove again to find that by reversing the grill fittings I could use the grill to cook and to boil water. This was a relief, as most of my remaining food would need a good deal of cooking.

With the ship driving through the fog close to her course, and with two large mugs of coffee and the remains of yesterday's curry inside me, the bright side of things began to filter through. I wrote more cheerfully:

"Estimated run to noon sixty miles. Strict water rationing and collecting every possible drop of rain water have eased the position a lot.

"I feel less timid at sea than I was. The essence of this thing is really to overcome difficulties as they arise. To do so brings a profound contentment and self-confidence extending far beyond the business in hand.

"There is no one to turn to for advice or to moan or squeal to. Therefore it requires little effort to tackle anything that goes wrong. It must be seen to, so you just get on and do it, and you find yourself doing things you would have thought impossible."

I sailed on through the fog, taking hourly echo-sounder readings. Sable Island radio beacon, away to the southward, gave an approximate position line showing that I was south of Nova Scotia, but there was no way of telling how far south. The sun and horizon had not been clear enough for sights for four days.

I had to overcome my great tiredness to change headsails as the wind waxed and waned. I tried again to estimate my position; but in the mental dullness of exhaustion I neglected the one important measure of laying off a bearing on the chart, north of which I must not go. So I sailed on through the silent, fog-shrouded world, all the time steadily closing the rock-bound coast of Nova Scotia.

At 1 p.m. we entered soundings once more. This was in order, as I expected to cross a series of offshore banks; but at 3 p.m. the depth had decreased to twenty-eight fathoms, which meant that, one way or the other, my estimated position must be out.

Now I plotted soundings every ten minutes; fifteen fathoms, twenty, fifteen again. Then the monotonous hoot of a foghorn began to starboard. Was it a ship? Or was not the sound being repeated too regularly? I dived below for the light list and tried unsucessfully to identify the signal.

I was still trying when a low rumbling which surged and receded became audible ahead. For a few seconds I did not realize what it was. Then I slammed the helm hard over and jumped for the foredeck to pull the genoa across as we swung round through the eye of the wind. As I wrestled with the sail, I knew the sound for what it was, and I glanced over the starboard quarter to where fifty to a hundred yards away through the fog I could see the lazy ocean swells heaping up and breaking in a frenzy of bursting surf against the iron-bound coast of Nova Scotia.

As we came about, the bolt holding the log inexplicably sheered and it disappeared, together with the rotator and line, leaving the outrigger still attached by its lanyard. There it lay in ten fathoms, as if it were an offering demanded by the strange gods of that gaunt coast. My knees were trembling as I stood tensed at the helm, for I had seen death that afternoon.

6

UNFRIENDLY COAST

"A tropical depression . . . became designated as 'Brenda' as it
moved up the U.S. coast, July 29–31."
                    —U.S. Dept. of Commerce Weather Bureau,
        Preliminary report of tropical storm "Brenda" : August 1960

*   *   *

"WARNING: This area is exceedingly treacherous, being
characterized by numerous shoals and tide-rips."
                            —Nantucket Sound: Esso Cruising Guide

BY 6.30 p.m. we were well clear of the Nova Scotian coast. The
visibility was still only a hundred yards, but *Cardinal Vertue* was
charging the seas and lifting to the swell of the open Atlantic. I
pressed on southwards and soon the foghorns of steamers traversing
the Canadian coastal shipping lane sounded ahead. We passed through
them in light airs until their faint echoes faded away astern.

Midnight found me writing: "Such a trusting little ship! She is
'chuntering' to herself and the kiwi as she bucks and fusses away to
the south-westward through the fog and darkness, outside all dangers
now.

"I don't want to let her down any more. After all she needs *some*
taking care of—come to think of it there are people on shore I would
rather not let down either!"

One final radio bearing on Sable Island and a glance at the echo-
sounder to make sure we were outside the forty-fathom line and I
turned in for two hours of badly needed sleep.

I awoke at 4 a.m. to find the night brilliant with stars and the wind
free so that I could lay course. For a time I stood in the cockpit nursing
a cup of coffee. Then as day began to break, high and red above a long
bank of cloud, I went forward and, holding on to the mast, gazed
upwards at the loveliness of the yacht's high sails, now tinged with
rose. I was thankful to be alive to see this dawn.

By a tremendous effort I stayed awake until I could obtain a sight

9. Four of the five race competitors at Plymouth before the start. *Left to right:* Francis Chichester, the winner, Blondie Hasler, Val Howells and David Lewis.

10. For the race, *Cardinal Vertue* carried 32 gallons of water, much of it in plastic bags stowed in the cockpit.

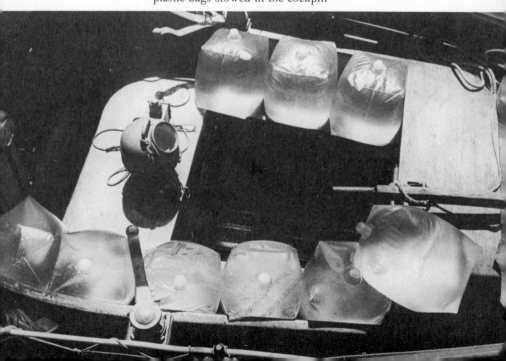

11. *Cardinal Vertue* in Plymouth Sound after the start of the race.

and then retired to my bunk, leaving *Cardinal Vertue* to dance through the sunshine across the blue, white-crested waves. That morning, July 25th, marked the end of my sixth week at sea; a week, as I wrote in the log, that was "not without incident".

Awakening that afternoon, I prepared to work out my morning's sight. The spare log which I had streamed off Nova Scotia was working well; the sight had been a good one—but it was useless. The deck-watch had stopped. In my exhaustion the previous night, I had omitted to wind it!

Would the radio, which was not working well, be able to pick up time signals from WWV, the U.S. Standards station at Washington? I tuned to 2,500 kc and listened anxiously through the headphones; nothing. No!—I could hear the faint voice of the Boston Marine radio operator forecasting calms. Well, I must try again at night, when sometimes reception is better. It was 2 a.m. before, to my infinite relief, the regular *toc, toc, toc* of WWV sounded, and I could start the deck-watch again. I resolved that in future I would compare it with my wrist-watch several times each day so as to have a stand-by time-piece whose exact error I knew. I was lucky to have obtained my time check when I did, for two days afterwards the radio gave up for good.

We seemed to have suddenly reached the south. It was warm for the first time for weeks. Next day, July 26th, we sailed across the Nova Scotia Banks about fifty miles off shore over a sparkling sea.

The metal spring which closes the clip of my safety-belt had rusted and snapped, so I bound the clip with thin shock cord to make a new elastic spring. This worked well for nearly four thousand miles, but I never felt quite at ease in trusting my life to such makeshift handiwork.

There was a relative absence of ocean swell on this windward side of the Atlantic, so I took advantage of the calmer weather to go aloft and put tape around the outer end of the damaged cross-tree and its shroud; it had not shifted an inch!

With a light favourable breeze we glided along under the spinnaker across lines of whispering overfalls. Later, the wind headed us, so I went forward to hand the spinnaker. This sail is set on a metal boom 11 feet long which, in *Cardinal Vertue*, pivots from the mast about 16 feet above the deck. When the sail is set, the boom is suspended horizontally. As I slackened the halyard and topping lift and pulled on the guy, the clip attaching the boom to the sail slipped, so that it swung down in an arc, crashing between my eyes.

I could not have been unconscious for long, because the blood which stained the blue spinnaker and white genoa had not yet clotted. Groggily, I finished lowering the spinnaker, hoisted the genoa and stumbled below. I was a little startled at the apparition reflected in the mirror; but wrote later in the log: "My nose has never been an asset and now that the bridge has been broken it may well be improved when the swelling subsides."

A week later I could summarize the incident. "From the distribution of the bruising tracking across the orbit three days after I cracked my forehead with the spinnaker pole, I apparently not only broke the nasal bone but also the frontal or sphenoid or both" (bones forming part of

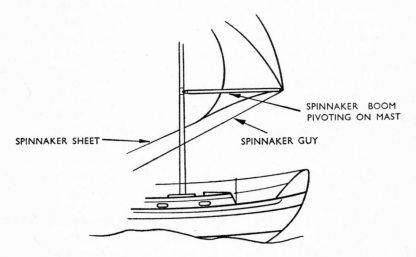

SPINNAKER BOOM
PIVOTING ON MAST

SPINNAKER SHEET ⟶

SPINNAKER GUY

the front of the skull). "I was easily tired for several days, possibly due to concussion, but the immediate effect, headache, wore off quickly after three aspirin—in any case I feel well enough now." It was a further week, however, before the abnormal tiredness had quite gone.

The remark that the headache "Soon wore off", was rather an understatement, for it does not tally with the log of the 27th. Due to light winds, I had to steer for most of the night following the accident, and how my head did ache!

But soon my attention was taken by the lights of a power vessel which had appeared ahead. For two hours, as she came nearer, she would yaw about showing first her green light then her red, so that I did not know on which side she would pass. At last all three lights began to glow steadily; she was heading straight towards me. I hastily came about and ghosted away with bare steerage way into the darkness to port, while she went blindly by, two hundred yards away, with diesel thumping and lights blazing.

Dawn broke clear, above the rippling overfalls, to show the first fishing boat I had seen since fog had closed in, south of Ireland. But I felt too ill to take an interest in anything except my own headache and the fact that I was chilled to the bone. So I climbed miserably between the blankets as the wind fell away into calm.

A good deal of thought had gone into making up medical kits and preparing a document to give advice to each competitor in the event of serious accident or illness. None of the drugs was needed, but neither were the distress flares; and I consider that carefully chosen medical equipment should always be carried on ocean passages in small craft. The aim is not first-aid, but fairly long-term treatment. For, especially if a man is alone, he must be able to treat himself and keep himself going for at least as long as it would take to reach a shipping lane; and that might be several weeks.

There are several ways of approaching this problem, which concerns a situation not dealt with by first-aid text-books. The document worked out for the race, and reproduced in Appendix Five, tries to make full use of modern antibiotic drugs and common sense.

On July 28th I rounded Cape Sable which was about forty miles to the north, and in light variable winds headed out across the Gulf of Maine towards Nantucket Shoals light-vessel.

A week before, Francis Chichester had won a well-earned victory by reaching the Ambrose Light.

Hasler was now within a hundred miles of his goal. He was writing: "Having a great time guzzling butter, jam, etc.—now unrationed!"

As Val Howells neared Bermuda his mood lightened. He had been worried at radio warnings of an approaching hurricane and even more seriously because his boat had been making far "too much water for comfort", and by July 26th things were so bad that he had written: "Will be glad to get to Bermuda (God willing)."

Jean Lacombe was bouncing about, far behind, in light contrary airs, somewhere between the Azores and Bermuda.

But I knew nothing of the others' progress. I was convinced that they would all be in New York already, yet this in no way diminished the thrill of getting out the last set of charts and setting my watch by Eastern Standard Time, five hours slow on Greenwich. I was making up on water too—if only the wind would hold!

Since the previous day delicate wisps of high cirrus and veils of alto-stratus had begun to spread over the sky from the westward. Now dark overcast, from which a fine rain was beginning to fall, hung over the sea, hiding the high clouds. The glass began to drop.

As the radio had gone dead, there could be no hints about approaching weather from Boston Marine, but it seemed fairly obvious that a depression was coming. "I will have to tack and reef and sail off course, but at least there will be no calms, and that is worth anything," I wrote.

But I was wrong. The expected "low" did not materialize. Instead the wind dropped right away as a day of disappointment ended in drizzling darkness and the slat, slat, slat, of the becalmed sails.

Midnight brought puffs of wind, which lasted for perhaps half an hour, before giving way to calm again. Later a new breeze would spring up from a fresh quarter only to die out in its turn. All night long, through warm, damp darkness, I steered and changed sails. Sometimes the genoa was needed, at others the spinnaker. The glass continued to fall very slowly.

With daylight came thick fog. I was on the foredeck changing sail when a deep throbbing sound became audible far off in the mist. I stood stock still, my scalp prickling with fear of the unknown. The noise was rapidly becoming louder and nearer. What strange machine could be racing over the water at such speed?

I ran back to the cockpit and sat clutching the useless tiller so tightly that my knuckles showed white, while my eyes strained fearfully into the mist. I was still sitting there when the rumble became an ear-splitting roar and a deluge of blinding rain thundered out of the sky. I have never known rain like it, even in tropical "cloudbursts". I made for the cabin, gasping, drenched and unable to breathe freely; thoroughly ashamed of my fear.

All day in thick fog we worked our way by soundings along the edge of George's Bank, about the middle of the Gulf of Maine. Lines of flotsam marked where currents met—seaweed, sponges, paper cartons, an empty life-jacket—for fifteen hours it was flat, glassy calm. Seagulls "under power" paddled past across that mirror-like surface where we lay helpless.

By midnight, constantly changing sail and steering in the light airs, I had made twelve miles headway in twenty-four hours. For some reason I began to feel less depressed for the remainder of the night, and even sang a little as I hoisted and lowered the spinnaker and adjusted the vane, and we crept onward through fog and drenching rain squalls.

Earlier in the evening I had been so sorry for myself, chafing at the calms and the lack of a compass light, and at my unpalatable food. Now I seemed to have snapped out of it—the slower our progress, and the further we were forced away from our proper course and north of Nantucket Shoals light vessel, the more did stubborn determination come to replace self-pity.

"The sea and winds certainly aren't letting me have this the easy way—but whoever expected that, or wants it?" I wrote then.

At midday on July 30th, the two-day fog parted to reveal a Wellsian structure of domes on stalks about ten miles away. This was Texas Tower No. 2, the first land-based object I had seen (except the Nova Scotia surf) since the lights of the Lizard and Ushant had dropped astern seven weeks before.

The sky cleared, but the glass which had slowly fallen from 1,021 mb two days before, to 1,009 mb, now began to drop so fast that in the next seven hours it fell 10 mb, to 999 mb. Such weather was outside all my experience. I read and re-read the weather notes in the American Pilot and the notes on gales off the Atlantic seaboard supplied by Bruce Robinson, Vice-Commodore of the Slocum Society. What could be coming? If only the radio were working! What a mercy for my peace of mind that it was not; for I was in the "dangerous semicircle" of tropical revolving storm "Brenda", which was now almost upon me.

These storms may or may not reach hurricane intensity (Beaufort force 12, sixty-five knots), and no such great wind velocities were recorded in "Brenda". But they can never be taken lightly. Under the heading "Tropical Revolving Storms" in the *Pilot*, is the ominous phrase — "while small vessels (for example, destroyers) have foundered". This line cannot fail to impress the crew of a yacht about the size of a destroyer's pinnace.

The storm came suddenly out of the south-east. At 5 p.m. *Cardinal Vertue* was still carrying full sail. Two hours later the mainsail was so close-reefed that it set badly. Everything had happened too quickly. Three times I had reefed; on each occasion late; another batten was gone; the phosphor-bronze snap shackle at the leach of the foresail had sheared. "Altogether a sorry performance!" I admitted in the log.

While daylight still lasted the clouds broke. Beneath a pale blue patch of sky we plunged to windward in the rising gale, over a green, white-capped sea, across an amphitheatre surrounded by tiers of great, tossing, black clouds. A stormy petrel was skimming the wave crests.

As the sun sank and the moon broke through the cloudwrack I stood on the transom gripping a backstay with each hand, heedless of fatigue, at one with my ship and with the gale; thrilling to the lift and scend as the yacht corkscrewed up and over the seas; every now and then lurching sideways with a breaking crest, or shuddering at the impact of a sea.

My recollections of the remainder of that night are hazy. The storm blew harder still out of a clear sky, and soon after midnight it began to veer, so that I could no longer lay the course for Nantucket light-vessel. The wind continued to increase, so I gybed onto the starboard tack and took in the foresail and lay-to under close-reefed main. But the main was set badly so at times it flogged, shaking the whole ship. According to Boston Weather Bureau Storm Advisory No. 6 of July 30th, the wind in the eastern semicircle within two hundred miles of the storm centre was 40 m.p.h., gusting to 60 m.p.h. I was at that time well in this semicircle, fifty to a hundred miles from the centre.

After all sail was stowed the yacht rolled violently up to twenty degrees to starboard and thirty degrees to port. The cabin lamp had gone out. Feeling sick and exhausted, I filled it with paraffin and lit it. Lowering sail and making all secure, heaving-to and filling and lighting the lamp, had occupied one and a half hours. For a time the fury of the gale increased but I felt too ill and tired to care.

It was still night when the storm left me as suddenly as it had come, to wreak havoc on the nearby coast. As far away as New York, Blondie Hasler who had just arrived, dared not leave *Jester*, even in harbour, for fear she might be damaged.

In pitch darkness making sail on that fantastically tossing deck was an even harder task than stowing it had been. I got under way in a strong south-west breeze; but by daylight I was becalmed once more.

For two days it remained calm. My first sights showed that we had been carried back by the storm and had since drifted up into the Gulf of Maine. No more should be said about these two days. They were one of the times when I was glad to be alone; for I showed up very badly—sorry for myself, depressed and miserable.

The second day of the calms was August 1st, the end of the seventh week at sea, a week during which there had been calms on every day. That evening a light breeze sprang up, still south-west, and I decided not to round Nantucket Shoals light-vessel, for we had now been set far to the northward and it lay fifty miles dead to windward. Instead, I would set course for Pollock Rip and take the tricky channel into the Sounds which lie behind Nantucket and Martha's Vineyard Islands. For all their tide-rips and shoals, this way would now be quicker. Luckily, I had brought detailed charts of the area to cope with this very eventuality.

At 2 a.m. on August 2nd I awoke and scanned the horizon and saw a flashing light on the starboard bow. A queer noise, rather like an engine blowing off steam, was audible at fairly regular intervals. The chart showed that there was a whistle buoy at Great Round Shoal, which was only a few miles north of my estimated position. Well, I thought, this must be it, ahead. I had never heard a whistle buoy before and the noise did sound most odd. But what else could it be?

Dawn was breaking, and soon by its light I could see two great wet backs, glistening, shot with gold in the first sunrays, come curving out of the water. The whales blew again, then side by side, swam off into the sunrise. So much for my whistle buoy!

Daylight showed a fishing boat not far away, so I altered course to intercept her. As I approached the motor fishing launch *Curlew* one of the two men aboard stepped out from the wheelhouse and waved.

"Good morning," I called. "Can you report me to U.S. Coast-guards, *Cardinal Vertue* out of Plymouth, England, bound towards New York?"

He nodded, replied, "O.K.", and turned back into the wheelhouse.

This casual reception took the wind out of my sails with a vengeance. And just when I was feeling like some budding Columbus! I hardened in the mainsheet viciously and shoved the helm over.

Across the water floated snatches of conversation from the wheel-house:

"That little bitty sail boat come all the way from Plymouth, New England."

"No. He said, Plymouth, *England.*"

There was a pause; then the wheelhouse door slammed open and a startled face appeared:

"Did you say Plymouth, *England?*"

"Yes, seven weeks out."

"Man!" over his shoulder to the mate, "This sail boat *did* come from Plymouth, England."

They told me that the light I had seen was Sankaty Head lighthouse on Nantucket Island. Great Round Shoal Channel lay ten miles to the north-west. I thanked them and set off again.

Five minutes later I heard the throb of an engine at full power and

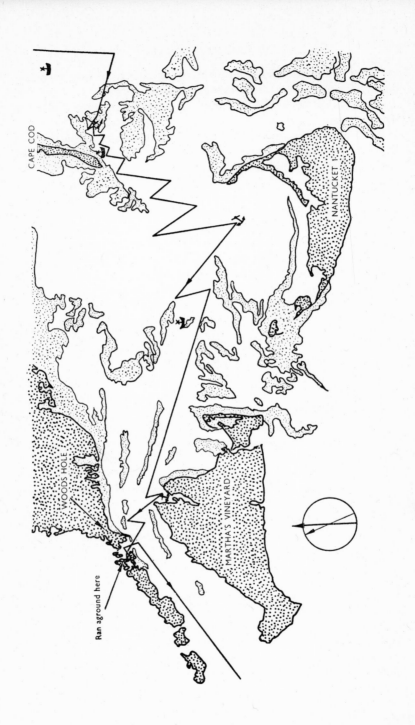

CAPE COD

NANTUCKET I.

WOODS HOLE

MARTHA'S VINEYARD

Ran aground here

looked round to see *Curlew* come surging up, her bow wave creaming high. She slowed alongside and a voice called:

"Did you come all the way from *England?* What sort of weather did you have? Here—you must want some fresh fish!"

It took real self-control to refuse this offer but the rules of the race laid down that we were not to accept stores from another vessel. "I am so damned sick of stew," I wrote in my diary, "and even the biscuit is nearly finished, but I am not going to get disqualified *now.*"

As I headed for Great Round Shoal buoy I studied the charts and tide tables but before we could reach the buoy, fog had set in. There was little chance of finding it now, so there was nothing else for it but to keep on until I could hear the fog signals of the two light-vessels which mark Pollock Rip channel, ten miles beyond the Round Shoal. I would miss the tide, but that couldn't be avoided. The only other course, to turn back and go round outside Nantucket Shoals light-vessel, fifty miles out to sea against light variable winds, was unthinkable when I could pass through Nantucket and Vineyard Sounds and then head direct for Long Island. So I watched the echo sounder and studied the charts. A tide rip showed white and broken in the mist to port, then was left astern.

"I will anchor and wait for the tide at Pollock Rip, if this wind holds and I can find it," I wrote. "What a pity the radio direction finder has packed up. But I am so happy to be doing something and getting places. My writing is worse than usual because I am trying to steer in an erratic wind and peer into the fog with fifty yards visibility, and listen, all at the same time.

"The tide turns foul at midday, and then all Nantucket Sound comes sluicing out of Pollock Rip channel which is bordered by shoals, overfalls and tide-rips."

By 9 a.m. I could hear Stone Horse light-vessel towards the inside of the channel and Pollock Rip light-vessel outside, both giving tongue.

The reasons for the decision I took then are recorded in my diary.

"Well, it is half-neaps; there should be enough water over the shoals; the weather is calm. Unless I can make use of the last of this favourable tide, I will have to anchor outside and not begin to negotiate the channel until after dark, with a headwind too. So I am heading straight in over the shoals through the fog, directly towards the sound of Stone Horse."

"God, it was tense!" I wrote afterwards. "Two hours with soundings in feet and the breaking water of the rips splashing aboard!

"Then the sound signals stopped. This could only mean that the fog was lifting around the light-vessel, but near me it was as thick as ever. Then I heard a bell—port side of main channel, bell buoys! I shouted aloud with relief, and a few moments later the low desolate outline of Cape Cod broke through the mist, fronted by a forlorn wreck. One by one the channel buoys loomed out of the fog.

"The tide was already streaming out of the Sound sweeping me back, so I anchored in six fathoms at 1.30 p.m. The tide raced past at 2.8 knots by the speedometer.

"So now the hook is down for the first time for two thousand, nine hundred miles, and I am finishing the gin, drinking to all those who made this possible."

While I was making things shipshape a small whale swam by. "What cheek," I thought—right beside Nantucket Island, the very home of whaling. There was only time for a hurried meal before the tide began to slacken. The wind had risen to force 6 and was blowing from dead ahead. I reefed 4 feet of the mainsail before starting to break out the anchor.

It took one hour and twenty-seven minutes to get that anchor in. Towards the end my hands would not grip any more, so I wound both arms in the chain and pulled by swinging my body backwards. My arms and legs were bruised and I ached all over.

By this time thick fog had descended once more. The wind was far stronger; a "smoking southwester" of force 7, which laid *Cardinal Vertue* far over as we tacked up the channel in sheets of spray, guided only by the blare of Stone Horse foghorn.

"I passed the light-vessel by sound—didn't see it though it was only a few hundred yards off; then hove-to and close-reefed the main and reefed No. 1 staysail," I wrote. "She carried all the sail she could bear even then, as the wind kept rising—force 7—maybe force 8; the fog thick as soup and night closing down, and we beating our way into the shoal-spattered waters of Nantucket Sound!

"What a night! The sea always has surprises and we are prepared to meet them all (except calms), but at each new one you think wryly— whatever can it cook up next?

"But it was wonderful! the challenge and thrill, dashing along like that!—and quite impossible without the echo-sounder.

"What a mess below! Every sail-bag had had to come out to free the anchor chain and now everything that is loose in the cabin is sent flying onto the sail-bags and the floor.

78

"As the wind rose, I had to gybe round at the end of each board, as she would not come about. Only once, at 7 p.m., when a buoy appeared, did I see anything other than fog and breaking crests.

"So by guess and by lead, we entered the Sound and headed towards the lee of Nantucket Island for one and a half hours. I was very much on edge because of an offlying shoal; there was no way of telling which side of it we were, or whether we were heading straight for it.

"At last we seemed far enough in. I got out the kedge anchor and warp this time, and at 10.10 p.m., threw it over in six fathoms, and sighed with relief because I was soaked to the skin and just about all in. The kedge held as well as a paperweight would have done!

"I didn't finally get the bower anchor's chain untangled and the anchor down until 11.30 p.m.—and could hardly walk then. I changed my sopping clothes and made coffee, and lay for an hour as exhausted as I have ever been.

"After the rest, I cleared the forepeak to have the lashing to hand which attaches the anchor chain to the Samson post, in case she started dragging ashore and I had to cut it quickly. Then I rigged up a handy-billy gadget which I hooked onto the chain over the bow to try to ease the terrific snubbing. By then the fog was lifting, so that I could confirm my position by lighthouses, and the wind had dropped to force 4 or 5.

"And now there is a pot of stew cooking and coffee warming up. Will I be fit enough to make use of the next favourable tide, which starts making at 4.30 a.m.? I rather doubt it."

But at 4.45 next morning I started to bring in the anchor. I had no winch and this time it was even harder than before. So I hoisted sail and lashed the tiller over. *Cardinal Vertue* would gather away, snub hard on the cable, bring up short and swing over to the other tack. This was the moment when, if I were quick enough, I could whip one turn of the chain round the Samson post. One turn at a time only, for after slackening momentarily, the chain became as taut as an iron bar. My hands were swollen and tender, my ankles cut and bruised by the chain, and my back was aching.

This last was my weakest point. Many years ago in New Zealand another student and I had spent ten days in a tent waiting for the weather to clear so that we could tackle an unclimbed peak. Conditions did not improve, but we could not bear to leave without making an attempt and set off up rocks which were plastered in wet new snow.

As the sun warmed the rocks and snow slides went sloshing down every gully we realized the danger and began to retreat. My companion was crossing a snow couloir, while I anchored him from the snow-covered rocks above with 60 feet of rope, when a snow avalanche buried him and swept him down the couloir, and the tightening rope plucked me off the rock buttress and flicked me through the air like a fly. I fell clear of the rocks and landed on my bottom on hard-packed snow near my companion, who had been cast aside by the avalanche in the lee of the buttress.

We crawled to safety, my friend clutching the head of his broken ice axe; thankful to have been spared the penalty for our foolishness. Our bruises soon healed, but ever since I have limped a little, and when parachuting during the war, would often feel an excruciating pain in my back. I dared not report this for fear of being thrown out of the Airborne Forces; but after the war I had by back X-rayed and found that in my climbing accident I had crushed a lumbar vertebra. So now if ever I flex my lumbar spine unwisely, the sciatic nerve gets trapped and a tiresome spell of hospital exercises, traction or manipulation and rest are required.

As I tugged away at the chain for an hour, wrapping it turn by turn around the Samson post, and then for another hour, I prayed that my aching back would hold.

At 7 a.m. a fishing boat came up and offered to help. I was sorely tempted, but the chain was nearly in.

"When did you get in here?" he asked.

"Last night, through Pollock Rip," I answered wearily, and he stared across at me in disbelief.

At 7.15 a.m., after two and a half hours' work, the anchor came in. Nantucket Island was still but a dim outline through the mist as I hoisted sail and headed up the Sound.

Then the mist rolled back to reveal a new world. Across sparkling green seas, white yachts were sailing on every hand. In the space of seconds we had passed from the grimness of fog and storm into something resembling the Solent during a sunny Cowes week!

I looked around at my untidy ship festooned with ropes and chain, and at myself, filthy, wet and unwashed, and reluctantly decided that I must clear up.

Soon a five-tonner came up with me, sailed by a pleasant-looking couple I would have liked to talk to. As I jumped eagerly up the companion ladder, I stubbed my toe and cursed aloud in anguish. A look of alarm and consternation spread over the two faces in the approaching yacht, which promptly sheered off and rapidly dwindled to leeward. I was left nursing my throbbing toe and the conclusion that I wouldn't be fit for polite society until I got over the habit of speaking my thoughts aloud!

When I unreefed, everything seemed to go wrong, even the topping lift came adrift and was only recovered after an unseamanlike struggle. Eventually things looked a little more shipshape, so after hurriedly shaving and changing, I could at last hoist the Blue Ensign without shame. Of course by now there were no yachts in sight!

In the early afternoon I entered Vineyard Haven on the last of the tide and anchored with the kedge in still water. A gaff cutter sailed by, which I thought for a moment might be Bruce Robinson's *Picket*. Yachts and fishing boats passed and waved or stopped to talk. A can of ice-cold beer was tossed across, which I had already drunk before I remembered the race rules.

I did not know it at the time, but only a mile inshore of where *Cardinal Vertue* was lying to her anchor, her famous sister, *Vertue XXXV*, was moored.

I was desperately tired, but with so many people to see and talk to I was too excited to sleep. I lay down and tried to relax, but was still wide awake when the tide began to make. At eight-thirty that evening I hoisted sail, hauled in the anchor and set off down Vineyard Sound, tacking against a light south-westerly breeze.

The night was clear with lights everywhere; lights of cars and houses and navigation buoys. I felt relaxed and contented, but had only had one hour's sleep since 2 a.m. two nights before, so that I did not notice when we sailed out of Vineyard Sound altogether and, swept by a four-knot tide, floated rapidly down the winding, sand-bank-strewn side-channel of Woods Hole.

At first I thought the echo-sounder must have gone wrong. Then I realized that we had somehow got out of the main Sound and I turned back. For one hour, then a second hour, I tried to retrace my course. It was after midnight now, the lights of the cars appeared at longer intervals as we crept through the darkness and I scanned each shadow hoping for clues as to our position. Then at 1 p.m. *Cardinal Vertue* slid to a halt and heeled over gently to starboard. We were hard aground.

7

AN END AND A BEGINNING

"This pretty young maiden she said unto me,
There's a fine full-rigged clipper just ready for sea."
—*Sea shanty*

I HAD no idea where we were. The torch showed a clear sandy bottom with the tide beginning to make. But on which side of the channel had we gone aground? The torchlight revealed that I had forgotten to lower the Blue Ensign, so I hurriedly threw it below out of sight. I had broken one record anyway; by crossing an ocean and running aground on the way! Jokes that we had made about Jean Lacombe's centre-board seemed in very bad taste. I could do with a drop keel now!

Overboard went the kedge anchor; down came the sails. Tables showed that the tide would soon be rising, but I must try to find out in which direction deeper water lay. I hauled a spare one-man rubber raft out of the forepeak, laboriously blew it up and, in the darkness, inserted the plug. Then I hung the riding light on a stay to guide me back and dropped my unwieldy craft over side.

Carrying the torch and compass, a chart and the frying pan, with which to paddle, I stepped gingerly aboard. As I pushed off the tide gripped the oval raft. I did my best with the frying pan, but the raft would spin round at every stroke so that we were being swept away by the tide. This wouldn't do at all! I turned back, but even though my paddling improved with practice, it was a hard struggle to regain the ship.

Just as we came alongside, an ominous hissing announced that all was not well aboard the raft. I hastily scrambled over *Cardinal Vertue's* rail, pulling my rapidly deflating craft after me. At daylight I discovered that there were *two* plug holes and that the cap closing one had not been secured. It had been adventure enough for that night and I decided to wait patiently for the tide to float us off.

At four in the morning, August 4th, when there was light enough to see that we were aground on a sandspit off a sleeping village, *Cardinal*

Vertue stirred and floated free. At almost the same instant the gentle south-west breeze gave way to a quickly rising wind from the north-west which now put us on a lee shore.

There was no time to waste; within minutes the sails were up and drawing and *Cardinal Vertue* was heeling over as the blast pressed her down. I flicked the anchor out of the sand as we passed and drew a sigh of relief as the echo-sounder registered 4, then 6 feet, of water under our keel.

When we were far enough offshore for safety, I reefed the mainsail and set off to find Vineyard Sound again. Four hours were spent in reaching it; and not until then did I know for sure where we had been, or on what we had stranded—Nonameset Island, Woods Hole, Massachusetts.

Back in the Sound once more, I was fascinated by a tide race which was tossing great showers of white water high into the air. I had never seen one so close before. It was not a sight to miss, so I altered course to close it cautiously.

A coastguard cutter, which had been cruising down the Sound, came over towards me to see if I was standing into danger. It was about to turn away again when I shouted across, requesting that I be reported to the New York Coastguards. I should have stipulated New York in my earlier messages for the report of my previous sighting by the fishing boat *Curlew* had not penetrated beyond Nantucket. This was only the second time since I left England that a report of my having been sighted reached New York and London.

While we ran down the middle of Vineyard Sound with a fair wind I was setting the ship to rights. Anchors, chains, spare sails, warp and rubber dinghy had to be restowed. Soon everything was in place, except for the kiwi racing flag which had impaled itself on the lightning conductor at the masthead. I felt rather sad about this, but prudently decided to postpone climbing the mast to free it until we were in harbour.

How good it felt to take final bearings of the land at 10 a.m., to stream the log and watch the hills drop astern, and know we were sailing safely out to sea once more.

"There doesn't seem to have been a soul about this morning," I wrote. "And I was away just as day was breaking—but no doubt some old retired Yankee whaling skipper was up and watching through his bedroom window, and shaking his head!"

The wind held, so that by 8 p.m., Block Island light was abeam, and at 10.30 Mauntauk Point light, on Long Island itself, was flashing over the starboard bow. There was no chance of sleeping for we were running before a most variable wind with the spinnaker set. From time to time we would sail through a rain squall, after which the wind would fall light for a spell.

Next afternoon, August 5th, we passed to port of two proud white liners and a bobbing champagne cork. At 3 p.m. the wind backed, so that the spinnaker had to come down; and borne by this new breeze, fog banks came rolling in. Ships were passing on every side now. From 10 p.m. to midnight we were becalmed, while their lights streamed past on either hand, like street lamps on a misty night. Then we were sailing again. At 3.20 a.m. the fog lifted to reveal a flashing light ahead. I went below, opened the log-book and wrote without emotion:

"Ambrose light-vessel, bearing 290° magnetic."

Then I stared at what I had written. For two whole years the Ambrose light had been the goal of the enterprise which had filled all my thoughts. "I don't believe it is real. I thought it was just a joke!" I said out aloud, and burst into tears. I could not stop crying for long during the next half hour. I would control myself for a few moments; then it would start again. I was still sobbing at intervals, when I rounded the Ambrose light-vessel at 4.59 a.m. E.S.T. on August 6th.

We had covered three thousand and twenty-four miles (three thousand one hundred officially) in fifty-four days' sailing time, fifty-six days since the official start of the race. On thirty-seven of those days there had been complete calms, whose combined duration had totalled seven days and fifteen hours.

Though I blew a foghorn and yelled, no one aboard the lightship stirred, so I signalled to a passing sports fishing launch and asked him to call up the Coastguards on his radio and ask them to tow me to the quarantine station, as it had fallen calm again.

We talked as I coiled in the log line and hoisted the Stars and Stripes at the starboard cross-trees. "Was I going to sell the boat there?"

"How will I get home if I do that?" I asked. There was a moment's surprised silence.

"You are *sailing* back."

"Yes."

"When?"

"As soon as I can repair everything—in a week if I can make it."

84

12. Francis Chichester's *Gipsy Moth III*, shortly after crossing
the starting-line.

13. Blondie Hasler's *Jester* away to a good start.

The skipper of the launch shook his head slowly.

"There'll always be an England!" he exclaimed.

Soon a Coastguard cutter came up. "That big yacht came in first," they replied to my eager questions, for nobody as yet had been able to tell me news of the race, "and we towed Colonel Hasler in from here a week ago."

"But when did the others arrive?" I demanded.

"Well, one broke his mast——"

"Yes, that was me, but the other two?"

"They haven't got in yet."

I could hardly believe it, not last after all, but third!

They took me in tow and soon we were racing past lines of buoys, innumerable fishing launches and half-submerged driftwood. We were going so fast that I dared not leave the helm. I was very tired now that reaction had set in, longing to sleep, wanting a meal and wishing above all else that I could leave the tiller to go forward to the "heads".

In my discomfort, it was without much interest that I watched the fabled skyline taking shape through the mist.

"I don't think much of skyscrapers," I thought, but as we came nearer I could see that these were only the gasometers on Coney Island.

I lapsed into lethargy once more, but roused when a high-speed motor launch came out towards us. The slim, blonde girl who was sitting gracefully on the foredeck with her wide skirt spread out over her ankles was waving. "Trust a girl to wave to a uniform!" I thought cynically, eyeing the trim Coastguard officers up ahead.

The girl reminded me of Fiona and I was overwhelmed by a sudden sick longing for her. If only she could have been here to share this moment with me! The undertaking, planned so patiently for two years, now seemed only an incident in my need to return to her. Even my discomfort was forgotten as I looked over with distaste and irritation at the girl on the speedboat who aroused such uncomfortable thoughts. I kept looking; gripping the tiller unheedingly, while she smiled at me and waved again.

No, it was impossible! I stared ahead once more, but after a moment, I had to turn back. There was Blondie Hasler, grinning from the speedboat's cockpit, and there on the foredeck was—Fiona!

The rest of that day is rather hazy and dreamlike in my memory. Fiona had borrowed the fare and flown to New York a few days before, to meet me. Blondie had called for her at her hotel that morning when the Coastguards had phoned to say I was at the Ambrose light.

At the quarantine station, thanks to Doctor Drescher, the port doctor, formalities were at a minimum. Even across the form headed "List of suspects aboard vessel", was written "Not even one"!

But for a full hour Professor Severinghouse of Columbia University put me through a fearsome psychological test designed by the U.S. space administration doctors. They were interested in our trip because, though they could make ground experiments on solitude easily enough, they could not reproduce fear. They were much too polite to say so, but they obviously also wanted to know whether observations on people like ourselves would also be applicable to really normal humans!

After this, an inventory was made of all the food remaining on board and I was weighed. I could hardly complain, as I had started all this, but I did wish that the American doctors were not quite so thorough. I had lost nineteen pounds.

The Dreschers were described by Blondie as "Running a Marina in which nobody is allowed to pay!" It is hard to find words to describe their kindness and hospitality. John Pfleiger, the Commodore of the Slocum Society, who took us to lunch, is another of the kindest people I have ever met; always unobtrusively ready to help. I had asked him for American charts and light lists before the race—to my embarrassment he would not allow me to pay for them.

Then a launch towed *Cardinal Vertue* to Sheepshead Bay, while a medical correspondent sat below, bravely going through my log and turning slowly green with the heat and unaccustomed motion. Meanwhile Blondie and I swapped experiences in the cockpit.

A number of ships had sighted him, including the *Queen Elizabeth*. There is an unconfirmed story that the officer on watch stared in disbelief and cried out "There's a bloody Chinese junk"; then went straight down below and swallowed half a bottle of whisky.

The other version, that on making his report he was clapped in irons for being drunk on watch, hasn't been admitted either.

When Blondie was in mid-Atlantic, a Russian deep-sea trawler, fascinated by the apparition, closed *Jester*. Her crew lined the rails calling and waving. Blondie's knowledge of the language is not good enough, however, for him to confirm or deny that they were shouting "Long live Mao Tse Tung!"

As we passed Coney Island and watched captive parachutes on

wires dropping from a tower we recalled our war-time parachute training, which we had both done at Ringway, near Manchester. "It all terrified me," remarked Blondie, quite untruthfully, I think. "None of the equipment had any adequate safety margin."

He told me about Francis Chichester's magnificent forty-day voyage and of how Val Howells had just reached Bermuda.

Then we were alongside the yacht club float at Sheepshead Bay, being welcomed by Tom Culyer, the Commodore. The men asked about gales. Their wives had no time for such nonsense; they were full of questions about Fiona. "Doesn't your girl friend trust you with us American girls?" one asked.

I have often been questioned whether the land "rocked" after fifty-four days at sea. The truthful answer, is that it did not; that is, until I had been introduced to a wholesome drink called "Kentucky Cream". Then it fairly heaved.

Next morning at high water we laid *Cardinal Vertue* alongside the club pier so that the propeller could be replaced at low water. I made her fast in what I considered to be seamanlike fashion, so that she would lean well in against the pier when the tide had fallen and left her high and dry.

Then Blondie, Fiona and I repaired to Bruce and Ellen Robinson's sixty-year-old gaff cutter *Picket* for breakfast. Bruce, who is Vice-Commodore of the Slocum Society, had become a friend through his letters before we had even met. He and Ellen had sailed out beyond Block Island hoping to meet me and escort me in, but I had passed them in the dark.

I will always remember that breakfast—pancakes, maple syrup and bacon. Every time Ellen asked if I would like more, I answered truthfully, "Yes". At length, to give Ellen a rest, Fiona took over the cooking until the stock of pancake mixture was exhausted.

We rowed to *Cardinal Vertue*, to find to my horror that she was leaning away from the piles, held only by straining warps attached to cleats which were beginning to twist under the strain of her four and a half tons.

"Do you always lay up your English boats that way?" a puzzled yachtsman asked politely.

"Yes, always," I replied firmly. "She is very stable."

Then I hurriedly made fast extra warps and prayed that they would hold.

Bruce and I replaced the propeller while Fiona scraped off what little weed and barnacles had collected, and filled the gaping seam which had caused the leak on the port side. The club members helped.

The weather was so heavy and humid that Fiona and I spent all our time on the yacht in swimming suits. We never could remember to put on shoes or more respectable clothes before passing through the clubhouse, but the good-natured club members came to make allowances for us. I was very glad to have remembered to bring some small yacht club burgees, which at least served as mementos for some of our new friends.

There was so much to be done; a Press statement to prepare, radio and TV interviews; magazine articles to be written, and so on. On arriving in New York, I had phoned Chris Brasher, *The Observer's* Sports Editor in London, and heedless of the bill the paper must be incurring, had excitedly told him my story. *The Observer*, besides providing the trophy for the race, had signed a most generous contract with the four English competitors in return for prior news rights. Modern publicity may be a nuisance but at least it helps anyone who is not a millionaire to recoup some part of his expenses on trips such as ours. Bruce Robinson firmly dragged me away from the boat next day to stay in his apartment to write and visit editors.

The Press were helpful and took pains to be accurate. The one exception was, I regret, an English correspondent who painted a picture of Fiona being carried off to sea by a pretty seamy character, as vicious as he was senile, who waded knee-deep through ex-wives! My daughter's stock at school had been slightly raised when her father had sailed the Atlantic. Needless to say this report was of far more interest and put it sky high!

Before the race we had made strenuous efforts to interest manufacturers in supplying us with free equipment. Apart from the Naval Life Saving Committe, a tool firm had been most helpful. My own prize came quite by accident. The invaluable echo-sounder which had been lent me was a new model not yet fitted with a waterproof casing. On my return, I wrote to the manufacturers asking whether a casing could be supplied before I gave back the set to its owner, and complimenting them on its performance. The manager promptly came to see me.

"It really *shouldn't* have worked all that time without the casing," he said, as he generously presented me with a new set!

Macklin Boettger, who owns a machine shop, welded my gooseneck and made me a new horse. He also arranged for the supply of some wonderful black bread which was sustaining and palatable and lasted all the way to Shetland. I was rather worried about the cost of the fittings, as he is a craftsman who made some of the gear for *Columbia*, the America's Cup winner; but he would not accept a penny.

Macklin's other ideas about food did not seem so practical as his special bread. One evening Ellen had cooked the largest steak I have ever seen. Macklin, who was dining with us, expounded:

"Protein!—poisonous!—forms rivers of toxic mucus!" meanwhile busily shovelling down forkfuls of "noxious" steak!

A week after my arrival, Fiona and I, who were temporarily acting for the Race Committee, were called-up by the Coastguards with a message that Val Howells had passed the Ambrose. After hurriedly phoning the Press, we took a cab to Statten Island Ferry and reached the quarantine station just as Val came alongside. His eyes lit up when he saw me, but after I had handed him his mail he stood balancing on his foredeck, heedless of all enquiries, until he had read the letters from his wife, Eira.

Then with Welsh eloquence he expressed the feelings which every small boat sailor must experience after an ocean voyage:

"Never again! I wouldn't so much as cross the bloody Serpentine in the *Queen Mary!*"

But not more than half an hour later, while his boat was being towed to Sheepshead Bay, and we were sitting in the cockpit drinking rum and eating popcorn, Val said thoughtfully:

"You know, for the *next* Single-handed Race I am thinking of trying a schooner. . . !"

Knowing he would be living close to nature all those weeks, Val had been sensible enough to bring with him a book about seabirds. One passage especially had impressed him.

"Look, I'll show you," he said, rummaging below for the thin volume, which he opened at the section on petrels.

"Mating takes place in a burrow, where for *one night only* in the year (Val's italics) is heard the special mating trill written as 'mmmm, mmmm . . . mm',", he read.

"Just think of it! One night in the year *only!*" He stared out to sea for a moment, overawed by the mysterious ways of nature.

His face darkened when we examined the broken gooseneck that he had repaired at sea.

"Yes there *were* bad times," he admitted. "I used to pray. Yes, I even prayed for you, David!"

"Thanks very much," I replied, nettled.

By this time Francis Chichester had become a veteran New Yorker and was busy writing a book about his trip.* Only Jean Lacombe was still at sea. He had been sighted in the Gulf Stream and was nearing the United States.

It was impossible for us to take advantage of all the hospitality that was so generously offered us, for there was much to be done in preparation for the return voyage and little time in which to do it. My own list of chores, prepared while I was still at sea, reads:

"Charge battery, get spare battery, repair engine, fit propeller, repair leak port side, repair gooseneck and clew fittings, new horse, check up on spreader, charts of Newfoundland and Shetland. New P.V.C. trousers. Fit stainless steel universal joint to self-steering gear. Repair cabin lamp. Repair radio. Gasoline, engine oil, torch batteries, books (borrow from Bruce)."

Among provisions I had specially included were: matches, cooking fat and butter, milk, candies, bread, ham, cheese.

During the fortnight we spent in New York, I was not even able to find time for a haircut. Fiona and Ellen Robinson went shopping efficiently and economically and the radio was repaired after a fashion.

The engine presented a bigger problem. Every electric lead had to be replaced. Damp and corrosion had wrought havoc everywhere. For days it was dismantled, reassembled and dismantled again. As I am one of those people whom engines do not like, I was fortunate in having the help of George Donaldson.

An American had remarked to me thoughtfully one evening, while we were crossing on the Statten Island Ferry towards the grandeur of Manhatten:

"Do you see the statue of Liberty there? When immigrants first see it they cry with emotion. After they have been a few days ashore, they cry again because everybody robs them!"

But my experience was exactly the opposite. For instance, George spent four evenings toiling over the engine after his return from work on the New York ferries. Sometimes he was aboard until well after midnight. Yet all that he would accept was a beer!

Before leaving England, Val Howells had arranged to sell his boat in the U.S.A. He lent me his P.V.C. trousers, as mine were ripped beyond repair, a spare log-line and rotator, and his safety-belt for

* *Alone Across the Atlantic.* By Francis Chichester: George Allen and Unwin, 1961.

Fiona, who was to accompany me on the first leg of the return voyage. He also let me have his surplus food.

Val's impromptu stop at Bermuda had been expensive, so I lent him half my money. I had been expecting to be paid in America for some radio and TV appearances but as the cheques did not turn up until later, in England, Fiona and I had to pool our resources and count our assets very carefully. We could not have managed without the Robinsons' hospitality.

There were several reasons why we must hurry our departure. The doctor who was looking after my patients must be facing an impossible strain for I had never anticipated being away so long. Fiona had to be in London to begin a course at a dancing studio in early September. She would have time to sail with me as far as St. John's provided we did not dally in New York, but she would have to fly the rest of the way from Gander.

"Late August is a bad time of the year for a small boat to be on the Atlantic," Humphrey Barton believes. Yet the very earliest I could hope to set out from St. John's would be the end of August. The route I proposed to follow led far north of the direct steamer lanes to Europe and close to the area of the maximum incidence of gales in the Atlantic in September, where they were about five times as common and far more severe than those usually encountered in August in more frequented parts of the Western Ocean.

But more than a thousand years ago, Norse longships had nosed into the creeks and inlets of Newfoundland, and they had come via Iceland and Greenland, too. I felt an overmastering urge to retrace the "Sea King's Road" from Newfoundland to the ancient Viking islands of Hjetland, which today are called Shetland.

However, even the Skald had chanted, "You cannot go in longships thither," when speaking of an autumn passage to the Faroes. So I must be on my way across the storm centre of the Western Ocean before furious, lashing seas should bar the way.

When, at last, we were ready to sail we had to delay our departure for two days while hurricane "Cleo" passed by. Fortunately, Sheepshead Bay, where we were moored, is a well-protected harbour and easily accessible from the open sea.

Val was experiencing difficulty in selling his boat. The first stock question would be:

"What make of motor have you?"

"None."

The intended buyer would be shaken, but if persistent would go on to the next.

"What's the cubic capacity of your ice-box?'

Again he had to confess the deficiency. Only a most serious yachtsman would put the third question.

"How far does your standing headroom extend forward of the mast?"

The reply that even the maximum headroom only just allowed you to sit usually ended the discussion. But a Texan who had reached this stage in the inquisition placed his hand on Val's shoulder and gently summed up his objections:

"That's a nice little boat you have there, son, mighty nice! But when I buy a boat I want full fornicating space below!"

We were unable to wait for the arrival of Jean Lacombe. He had radioed his position to the Coastguards when he approached Nantucket. As the hurricane was also heading that way, they sent a cutter out to him which gathered him in out of harm's way until the danger had passed.

One remarkable feature of Jean's voyage is that a keg of whisky which had been given him in Plymouth remained unopened. Val helped him remedy this deficiency. In a letter to me Jean wrote:

"Feelings were just the same as on land, too much to do to feel lonesome!"

He had been sighted twice while crossing the Gulf Stream. On the second occasion the steamer *Christopher Columbo* had come alongside to ask if he required help. He had waved his arms and replied in French that all was well. There was nothing unusual about this incident, except that Jean flatly denied that it had happened at all. Nobody took any notice of this, as he could be expected to have been rather "boat happy".

But on November 6th, forty-nine-year-old Daniel Gautier in the seven and a half metres sloop *Isis*, reached New York, a hundred and fifty-nine days out from St. Nazaire:

The mystery of the sighting by the *Christopher Columbo* was now explained, but who could have expected two Frenchmen to have been at sea in the same area at the same time, both in tiny sloops?

The Dreschers and John Pfleiger did their best to look after Gautier.

"Like most single-handed sailors," Pfleiger wrote, "he is a timid and mild-mannered man—five years in a German concentration camp, a tiff with the French Government who put him in St. Anne (the crazy asylum) have left their imprint—he came as it is, without a passport, much money or anything."

In spite of the efforts made on his behalf, Gautier was deported back to France.

After two weeks in New York, Fiona and I set out from Sheepshead Bay in the late afternoon of August 20th. We were flying the Stars and Stripes from the starboard yardarm, with below it, the flag of New York State and the Sheepshead Bay Yacht Club burgee. Our Blue Ensign waved astern. In the cabin hung a plaque from the Slocum Society, inscribed "Third Man Home".

Such a host of craft escorted us that we were terrified lest we should hit one. Launches and speedboats raced round us, horns blaring; yachts and sailing canoes zigzagged by. We missed them all, though later Blondie was not so lucky! Then at last we were alone, outward bound over the lift and surge of the swell as we curtseyed past the Ambrose light-vessel in mist and darkness.

Jean reached New York the next day and with his arrival the first Single-handed Transatlantic Race was over.

The results were:

Francis Chichester: 40 days
Blondie Hasler: 48 days
David Lewis: 56 days elapsed time from official start (54 actual time)
Val Howells: 63 days elapsed time (55 days actual time)
Jean Lacombe: 74 elapsed time (69 actual time).

Chichester's feat was one of unrivalled courage and tenacity; he well deserved his splendid victory.

With his battened lug rig and the many other innovations on *Jester*, Hasler, I think, made what is perhaps the biggest contribution to ocean sailing for thirty years.

A week after our departure he set out for the Hamble where he unobtrusively picked up his mooring the day after I reached Lerwick. His time at sea, thirty-eight and a half days, was exactly the same sailing time as my own. Later, Chichester and his wife also sailed home, via the Azores.

But the contagion had spread. In the early winter, Bruce and Ellen Robinson abandoned their Madison Avenue apartment, and with *Picket* loaded down well below her marks, set off along the coastal waterway for Florida and the West Indies. Bruce ends a letter in which he describes storms, running aground on sandbanks, violent tides, running aground in rivers, bitter cold, running aground in canals: with a note saying that they were "having the time of their lives".

But now in late August *Cardinal Vertue* was heading north and east, towards where I knew, with trepidation but with a strange fascination as well, that I was to challenge the great winds of the Northern Sea.

8

TO BRING ME OMEN

These effigies of grief moved
Like refugees over the water;
The icy empresses of the Atlantic
Rising to bring me omen.
— GEORGE BARKER

THE strategy of our homeward passage was to sail well offshore to take advantage of the steadier winds of late August, and if possible to be helped along by the Gulf Stream; but not so far out that we could not reach shelter in the event of a hurricane warning being broadcast. We therefore aimed to head a little south-of-east until Nantucket Shoals light-vessel was abeam to port, then turn north-of-east along the northern edge of the Gulf Stream, passing outside Sable Island and making our landfall at Cape Race, Newfoundland, just over one thousand miles from New York.

The temperature was near the eighties and sultry. We kept a cotton pullover near the companionway, as the one on watch on deck at night sometimes felt chilly. Apart from this, Fiona wore only her bikini, and I my swimming trunks, day and night.

The vane was set to a good quartering breeze which drove us through the heat-haze. Though we were sailing one of the busiest sea lanes in the world, not a ship did we see during the first two days.

We left Sheepshead Bay at 6.30 p.m. (Eastern daylight time) on August 20th, and by midnight on the 22nd we were passing Nantucket Shoals light-vessel. Only two things marred the perfect peace of those days; myriads of biting flies, and Fiona's seasickness. Once Nantucket shoals were astern the sickness left her, though she was still weak from lack of food. In spite of the lively lift with which *Cardinal Vertue* was corkscrewing over the waves, she decided to have breakfast. What would she like?

"Pancakes, maple syrup and bacon, please."

I groaned and set to work. The ship was jerking so violently that

95

the frying pan soon tossed the pancakes into small piles of blackened debris, the maple syrup spilt, the bacon was burnt. I handed over the unsavoury mess and watched, revolted, while Fiona ate it with relish.

"Whatever is the matter?" she asked solicitously, suddenly noticing my face.

"Damn it to hell, *I'm* seasick now!" I snapped.

Now that Fiona felt better, she began to tackle the problem of finding her sea legs. This required determination, for although as a dancer and rock climber poise and balance are second nature to her, balance is of little use aboard a small bucking yacht, where you must always hang on or wedge yourself securely. Quick moving and impatient Fiona took another two days to adjust herself to this irksome routine; meanwhile she was thrown heavily again and again until she was bruised and sore all over.

But once she had learned to cope with the motion she soon became adept at rolling up the mainsail, changing headsails and managing the vane. She had mastered the traditional skills of an able seaman—to hand sail, to reef and to steer.

We ran one hundred miles on our first full day at sea, ninety on the second; then a weak depression which had been forecast by cirrus cloud and Boston Marine Radio, headed us, so that we only made sixty-seven on the third. That day the wind rose to thirty-four miles an hour, force 7.

The sea these days was a deep vivid blue. Sooty storm petrels, Leach's petrels, kittiwakes and guillemonts flew around us. I knew their names this time as I had been lent Val's precious book.

Once a school of porpoises in line abreast charged out of the face of a wave. Fiona waited patiently with her camera for them to do it again, while I told her not to waste time, for they would have swum miles away. Then out of the spume of the wave-crest, still side by side, they arched into the sunlight once more. Fiona clicked the shutter and replaced her camera without comment.

The next day, against headwinds, we made good only fifty-eight miles, but the following run was ninety-five, and on the day after, August 27th, the last day of our first week at sea, we made our record run of one hundred and twenty-four miles. After a week in which there had been only half an hour of calm, New York lay six hundred and thirty miles astern.

The previous day the log line had parted and gone to the bottom together with the rotator. I decided not to stream the spare one but to keep it in reserve in case of prolonged fog. For the moment we were getting sun sights every day, as well as radio time signals when required, so navigation was easy.

Each day we ran the engine for twenty minutes or so to charge the battery and keep it in trim. To conserve electricity we did not use the navigation lights unless a steamer passed near. One night a coastguard aeroplane picked us up on radar and circled us closer and closer. I deliberately kept the lights off, wondering if he could find us. Sure enough, as he banked overhead, he switched on a searchlight which picked us up immediately.

Ships appeared frequently, often only a few miles away, but they did not see us and the danger of collision was vividly brought home to me one night. I was writing up the log and looking out at intervals; the weather was clear and the visibility good; I had scanned the horizon no more than half an hour before. Suddenly the cabin was illumined by a blaze of lights as a liner raced by at twenty knots only three cables to port.

We still had many things to do for which there had been no time in New York. For instance, only now did we have leisure to open the last of our mail. The prize find was a poem. A friend of mine, with apologies to Lewis Carroll, had produced a magnificent sea-epic which could not be rivalled by even the most technical bar-room discussion in a very nautical yacht club.

A Luff Lyric of Vertue and Boaty
by Merton Naydler

'Twas Plymmig, and the beamsey sheets
Did gybe and spinnake o'er the beach,
All burgee were the mizzen beats
And the stay tack outreach.
Beware the jurygaff, my son,
The cleats that jam, the shrouds that stretch,
Beware the trimaran, and shun
The clumptions cataketch.
He took his tiller luff to deck
Long time the distant main he sought,
So ruddered he by the gallefry
And anchored there athwart.
But as in clewsome fend he keeled
The cataketch with forestay guide
Came riding through the gale and heeled,
All reefed upon the tide.

About! About! and in and out
The plimsoll mast went log-a-smack!
He left it barred, and planing hard
He jibbed, abafting back.
"And hast thou slooped the cataketch?
Port to my helm, my boomish buoy!
O freeboard horse! O transom course!"
He portled in his joy.
'Twas Plymmig, and the beamsey sheets,
Did gybe and spinnake o'er the beach,
All burgee were the mizzen beats
And the stay tack outreach.

My last haircut had been in London nearly three months earlier.
While I had been able to trim the front and sides with scissors and my
neck with a razor, the back had grown ever longer and more shaggy.
"I am going to do something about this now," announced Fiona
one day, eyeing my coiffure with displeasure. A mattress could have
been stuffed with the result of her efforts!

We did not steer by hand except when the breeze was too light to
work the vane, otherwise the kiwi was left in charge. It was only when
there was a strong wind and big seas from the quarter that the power
of the waves tended to overcome the strength of the vane and broach
the ship to. I learned later that this could be completely cured and the
ship would sail just as fast if I lowered the mainsail and kept on under
the genoa. For this was a larger sail (230 square feet against the main's
180) and as it set further forward than the mainsail, it had much less
tendency to drive *Cardinal Vertue* up into the wind.

When I awoke and went on deck to take over my watch on the
afternoon of the 27th, the ship was broad-reaching over blue white-
capped seas before a force 6 breeze. Some porpoises were playing to
starboard and a tiny sooty petrel danced over the foam flecks in the
sunlight. But where was the mate? For a moment I knew panic; then
I came upon her, dressed in her blue bikini, curled up in the lifebelt on
deck, eating popcorn!

That evening, steep phosphorescent seas nine to ten feet high came
combing up astern before a wind of thirty-four to thirty-six miles an
hour, which sometimes gusted to force 8. Once we were pooped by a
breaking crest, but only foam and spray splashed into the snug cabin
where Fiona was cooking.

Next day we began to cross Banquereau Bank in soundings. To the north of us heavy fog shrouded desolate, treacherous Sable Island, a twenty-mile crescent of sand, which lies ninety miles off the coast of Nova Scotia. A misty horizon had prevented me from obtaining reliable sights; and just as it had done some weeks before, the radio beacon on Sable Island was giving misleading bearings. On that occasion I had been nearly wrecked on Nova Scotia, but this time we aimed to keep east of the Island. The relevant paragraph in the *Nova Scotia and Bay of Fundy Pilot* was not too encouraging. It says:

". . . the irregularity of the currents and tidal streams in the vicinity of Sable Island is probably one of the principal causes of the numerous wrecks that have occurred on the island . . . but . . . their general trend is to set to the westward; many vessels wrecked on Sable Island supposed themselves to have been considerably eastward of the island when they ran on shore."

Study of the pilot chart only seemed to show that the currents converged on the damned place from all directions! It was also a notorious neighbourhood for fogs; so altogether this was an uncomfortable spot to be without sights, and for radio bearings to be at odds with the estimated position. I began to be touchy as we ran through the darkness; nor was I much cheered to see the pale greenish glow of the Aurora arching across the sky to the northward shortly before dawn.

August 29th. There was still no sight obtainable. According to our dead reckoning we should be well past Sable Island, but radio bearings persistently came from abeam. I decided to discard the radio bearings in plotting our course, but to keep an alternative set of positions based on the assumption that they alone were correct. In either case, unless the wind changed, we would soon pass clear.

About 3 p.m. *Cardinal Vertue* tripped in her stride as the forefoot struck something with a resounding thump. I sprang into the cockpit in time to see a long greenish body just awash, spinning in the wake astern—a dead porpoise or small whale, we thought it.

Two hours later, when Fiona was finding sunbathing a trifle chilly and had donned a pullover, we sighted a small vessel ahead. As we approached, we saw that she was a strange-looking fishing boat, *Janet Irene*, from Liverpool, Nova Scotia. She closed us in the gathering dusk, and hailed to ask where we were heading.

"St. John's, Newfoundland."

"We thought you must be on that course," was the comforting reply.

"What *is* that thing on your bow?" I asked, overcome by curiosity.

"That's for spearing swordfish, but they're getting pretty scarce here this time of the year," came the reply.

During the night the wind backed and increased. I was adjusting the vane when the metal clip on the foreguy sheared and the boom gybed all standing. No damage had been done, but the change in wind direction was forcing us northward, towards where, if the radio bearings were correct, destruction lay waiting in the surf breaking on the drying banks, east of Sable Island.

I became more tense and irritable every minute as I watched the echo-sounder readings and studied the chart over and over again.

It was nearly midnight when I decided to play for safety. By now it

was blowing twenty-six miles an hour, force 6, so before wearing ship on to the other gybe, the genoa had to come in and the main be reefed. The mate steered and tended the sheets, while I struggled on the wet deck in the darkness, and in my worry about our position I cursed her most unjustly, until she was almost in tears.

Neither of us had eyes at the time for the wild beauty of the soaring searchlights and curtains of cold unearthly fire which now began to pulse into life across the northern sky, springing up, arch upon eerie, glowing arch, to reach the very zenith.

Fiona forgave my bad temper when I told her how worried I had been in case we were standing into danger, but I had shaken her confidence in her own seamanship, and this took some time to return.

It was not long before we left soundings on reaching the edge of the Nova Scotia Banks and sailed on over deep water. We need not

14. Val Howells, "The Bearded Viking", takes *Eira* across the starting-line at Plymouth.

15. *Cap Horn*, Jean Lacombe's 21-foot plywood, centre-board sloop, which was a late starter but completed the course in 74 days.

have worried. Our dead reckoning had been right after all and the radio bearings inaccurate.

But there was a deeper reason for the anxiety that had been reflected in my snappiness. All at once we had left summer behind; we had felt the first cold breath of the winter stealing upon us from the northern wastes and Arctic seas, bring me omen of what lay ahead.

Long into the night I pored over the pilot charts. Yes, the percentage of all ships' observations in the Atlantic during which winds reached force 8 and above, rose steeply in September. In the western approaches of the Channel, the July figure was 1–2 per cent., August 1–3 per cent., September 2–4 per cent. But I was bound far to the northward of the Channel, across the stormiest stretches of the whole Western Ocean, and here the gale percentages for September read 5, 7, 9 and 7, until north of the 60th parallel and east of the Hebrides, they fell to 4.

In the early hours of the morning I wrote in the log: "Yesterday Fiona was still wearing her bikini, and I my trunks, but to-night and the night before, the pale lights have been flaring to the northward. Orion hangs high and clear now; and it is a winter constellation. The sun's northerly declination is down to 9 degrees, soon it will sink past the Equator into southerly declination. Signs, all signs, to hurry on. Summer is ending and I am bound towards 60° N, east-north-east over two thousand miles of ocean. Best not to linger overlong!"

On we sailed, north and east through a grey dawn beneath the overcast, to log ninety-eight miles by noon. Later in the day the wire burgee halyard chafed through. Fiona caught a glimpse of the brilliant colours of the Royal Burnham Yacht Club burgee floating tantalizingly close as we drove by, running before the wind with the mainsail boomed right out and pinned by the fore-guy. By the time we had sheeted in the boom and gybed, and headed back to search fruitlessly among the waves, it had disappeared.

The same thought was in both our minds as we came back onto our course once more and hoisted the Little Ship Club burgee on the spare main halyard—the difficulty of picking up a man overboard.

At 6 p.m. we entered soundings once more over St. Pierre, westernmost of the Grand Banks of Newfoundland. Here we crossed my outward track of July 21st.

During the past few days Fiona had occasionally noticed a curious feeling that a third person was on board. The sensation was of a somewhat neutral presence, neither friendly nor hostile; momentarily so real that she would begin to turn round to speak to it. When we compared notes we found that our experience was identical. In my case it usually occurred when I had just awakened and was going on watch. What is the explanation? I do not know, but this is a very common experience in the wilds. Perhaps we are so used to other people around us in everyday life that our senses reflect some echo of their former presence, even when they are not there.

That night the aurora flickered once more. Next day, August 31st, Cape Race radio beacon became clearly audible, sixty-five miles away. Unlike Sable Island it gave an accurate bearing.

As it grew dark again the wind fell light and we had to steer. So silently did we slip forward that we caught a flock of roosting seabirds unawares, until suddenly the air was filled with alarmed, indignant, squawks as they flapped away.

At 4 a.m. on September 1st, a flashing light appeared on the port bow, so I thankfully handed over to the mate, with instructions to call me when she sighted land. I was very soon awakened, when daylight showed the slate cliffs of Cape Pine.

We rounded Cape Race before noon and headed north up the coast with a fair wind. We passed within a quarter of a mile of the famous Cape, which towered across the cold green water in tiers of slaty ledges, backed by barren country. As we went by, mist shrouded the promontory and a fog signal began to blare.

But the land mist gradually cleared until we were sailing up a corridor between the coast on our port hand and a wall of dense fog which hung over the Grand Banks to starboard.

I wished to make all possible speed because the glass had begun to fall quickly, and cirrus cloud spreading from the west foretold an approaching depression.

We tore along through the calm water in the lee of the land, quickly eating up the sixty miles that separated us from St. John's. Bare, rounded hills ended abruptly in great sweeps of stratified cliff. Gullies and sheltered slopes were clothed with pine forest, while at long intervals at the head of some deep inlet there would be a scatter of white houses.

As I sat at the tiller I mused on the "courageous captains" whose schooners had faced the fog, ice and storms of the Grand Banks over the centuries. Where were they now? I feared that, along with the caravelles and longships, they could dwell only in that hall of memory which enshrines the quiet heroism of man. It would have been about this time in the evening that the smaller schooners from the outports would have come sailing out of the rolling fogbanks to seaward, to head for land; booms squared off, brown sails drawing as they ran towards home.

It was a moment before I realized that the four schooners which had just materialized out of the fog were real. On they came; small craft, 30 or 40 feet long. One, towing a dory nearly as long as itself, crossed our bow and disappeared shoreward behind two fantastic rock pinnacles called "The Hares Ears", to enter Fermeuse Harbour.

Near this spot, seventy-seven years ago, a man rowed a dory in from the Grand Banks. His companion sat rigid and ice-sheeted in the stern, where he had been frozen to death.

On January 25th, 1883, Howard Blackburn and Tom Welsh had

been fishing in one of the dories from the schooner *Grace L. Fears*, about one hundred miles off the Newfoundland coast. A storm drove them to leeward in fierce snow squalls, and all through the night and next day they had to bail and chip away frozen spray. Sometimes they tried to row, but usually they had to lie to an improvised sea anchor as their little kedge anchor dragged. Blackburn lost his mitts, so that his hands began to freeze. He bent his fingers over and poured water over them so that they froze into talons which could still grip the oars. Tom Welsh died that night and Howard Blackburn rowed for another day and a half before he sighted land. He had spent three days and nights in the dory without food or water.

As he lost all the fingers of both hands and a half of each thumb, Blackburn had to give up fishing. To enliven his retirement he had a 30-foot sloop built in which, sixteen years after his ordeal, he sailed alone from Gloucester, Mass., to Gloucester, England, making the crossing in sixty days. Not content with this feat, he set sail once more from Gloucester, Mass., in 1901, in a still smaller sloop, the *Great Republic*, only 25 feet long. Again this man without fingers was entirely alone. He reached Portugal safely in thirty-nine days.

After darkness had fallen on September 1st, I wore ship onto the starboard gybe in order to keep well offshore, for lights, either for navigation or of houses, are rare along the Newfoundland coast and the weather was rapidly deteriorating. Then, after putting our watches forward one and half hours to Newfoundland summer time, I handed over to Fiona and turned in.

About 3.30 a.m. on September 2nd I came on watch again to find that Cape Spear light was winking to port. We gybed again and, well reefed, ran towards the land, sweeping in across impressive rollers. Soon mist closed down until we had only a fog signal to guide us.

The wind had gusted up to thirty-four miles an hour, force 7, and our lee rail was pressed under as we raced into calmer water in the shelter of the dim, misty, outline of Cape Spear. Ahead towered a red limestone cliff, split by a monstrous gash, which was flanked on the one hand by an old fort and on the other by a lighthouse. This was the entrance to St. John's Harbour, the most magnificent landfall I had ever seen.

As we entered the narrows, rain was thundering against the rock ledges above and drumming on the painted wooden houses, fish-drying frames, anchored dories and *Cardinal Vertue*. But all wind was cut off by the walls of the defile, so that the sails slatted uselessly.

Soaked to the skin, Fiona lowered sail while I started the motor, and we set off round St. John's harbour in search of a mooring. It was only 7 a.m. and no one was about. Even in this sheltered basin squalls made the leeward piers unsafe. We eventually moored at a coal pier at 7.30, ahead of a Bowring sealer, two trim Icelandic trawlers and an incredibly rusty Spaniard, which had spent all summer on the Banks. We had covered one thousand, one hundred and thirteen miles in twelve and a half days.

We found a better mooring in the afternoon, at one of Bowring's wharves nearer the town beside some sadly cut-down Grand Banks schooners which were now coasters, trading with the outports.

Groups of quiet fishermen and seamen came to look at our boat. This was embarrassing as our deck was a jumble of sails and ropes, and I knew the knots with which I had made fast the warps were not the correct ones. Nor could we afford to buy a Newfoundland or Canadian courtesy ensign. The professionals eyed our slender spars with some mistrust. But I was glad to hear that their opinions were, on the whole, favourable.

We had eaten so well on the trip from New York, thanks to Fiona's cooking once she had had her sea legs, that we now had partly to re-stock the ship.

The grocer had various brands of margarine, canned goods, sweet biscuits and salt cod; Fiona always chose the cheapest. At length he entered into the spirit of the thing and began to hunt out long-forgotten cans from dusty back shelves.

Leaving Fiona only enough money for her hotel bill and the journey to Gander, we spent the remainder on food for me, a post card to Tom Moncrief in Shetland, and rather meagre presents for Barry and Anna. "Be sure and bring me back lots of Yankee chewing gum," Barry had written; and chewing gum was all his father was able to bring him.

A mission launch, which came alongside on Sunday, gave us a pile of books and Canadian magazines, a welcome supplement to those we had borrowed in New York. In the end, I had everything I needed, except that I could not afford enough paraffin. However, the engine was working and should be able to charge the batteries so that I could use electric light. When I did leave St. John's, the currency on board totalled one cent Canadian!

We had arrived in Newfoundland at the beginning of a public holiday and how we blessed the peace and quiet. Derick Bowring, whose family of merchant adventurers have been the owners of fishing schooners and sealers for generations, took us to dinner one evening at his home above the town. Before the meal he drove us up Signal Hill which rises to 500 feet on the northern side of the narrows. The town and harbour were spread out beneath us. Then I turned and looked out over the Atlantic stretching on and on to the rim of the night, and I thought how peaceful it looked. Yet it seemed to me that this apparent peace concealed such forces as would test my resolution to the utmost; I thought of the morrow when I must sail, and I was afraid.

But a Vertue is a confident little ship, and has good reason to be so. Speaking at a dinner the previous winter, Jack Giles, their designer, had said, rather piously I thought, that a hand "other than his own" had guided his pencil when he drew the lines of the first Vertue, *Andrillot*, in 1936. Later the same evening, he said more confidentially,

"As a matter of fact, old man, someone asked me to make him a miniature Bristol Channel Pilot cutter, so I just copied the underwater lines." This confirmed, and rather amplified, his earlier remarks.

In keeping with their descent from such a famous English line, Vertues are heavy displacement craft by modern standards; for $4\frac{1}{2}$ tons displacement on a 21-foot waterline is a good deal. It implies a comparatively easy motion, more room below, more speed in light winds because of a small wetted area, but more strain on spars and rigging due to the greater momentum imparted by the heavy hull. Two tons of the weight is made up of lead in the keel, so like all yachts with ballasted keels, Vertues are self-righting in the event of a knockdown; always provided that the upper works remain intact and waterproof.

The class was given its name after *Epeneta*, in 1939, won the cup donated by M. B. Vertue to the Little Ship Club for the best cruise of the year. Hence the spelling of Vertue. As I was writing the last sentence, I looked at the Vertue Cup more closely, to find with some amusement that the recipient for 1960 had been misspelt *Cardinal Virtue!*

When she was being built at Christchurch in 1948, her original owner suggested calling her *Easy Vertue*. Mr. Elkins, her builder, was scandalized.

"It would be more appropriate to name her after one of the five cardinal virtues," he admonished severely; and so *Cardinal Vertue* she became.

Since *Vertue XXXV's* passage to New York in 1950, Vertues have been as thick as flies upon the Atlantic. In 1952 Dr. Cunningham crossed from Ireland to the West Indies in *Icebird*. In 1955 he sailed from Newfoundland to Bermuda, and in 1957 from Bermuda back to Ireland.

In 1955 David Robertson reached the Bahamas from England in *Nan*. This yacht was originally named *Jonica*; her next owner called her *Easy Vertue*; David Robertson changed her name to *Nan*. Her present owner has called her *Jonica* again.

Next year, John Goodwin in *Speedwell of Hongkong*, which Peter Hamilton had already sailed from Singapore to England, set out from Gibraltar to the West Indies. Two years later he left the West Indies for Brazil and, ultimately, Capetown.

Then in 1957 Peter Hamilton in *Salmo* became the second single-hander to reach the New World by the northern route. He laid up at

Quebec, and the following year continued on his way, with his wife as crew. They traversed the Panama Canal and crossed the Pacific to Tahiti, finally returning to California.

The record is an honourable one, and if any small yacht was fit to meet the September gales of the northern wastes of the North Atlantic it was a Vertue; and *Cardinal Vertue* was now in superb trim.

It seemed a far cry now from when I had bought her in 1959 and asked Humphrey Barton's advice about how best to install a self-draining cockpit with the least expense. He had written back to say that one was unnecessary round the English coast. After receiving my reply, he 'phoned me. Where was I going anyway?

"To Southend Pier, it gets *very* rough there!" I replied shortly.

"Oh, of course, then you *will* need a self-draining cockpit," he replied immediately. Understanding had been established.

The winter of 1959 had seen an incredible number of jobs accomplished and Bob and Sunny Coles of Tucker Brown's, in particular, must have hated the very sight of me. Yet their good temper and helpfulness had never varied. But when we were finally launched and I promptly ran aground opposite their yard, Bob had shaken his head and muttered, "He'll never make it!"

But I must not delay longer. The morning of September 5th was bright with sunshine and a fair wind rippled the blue, red and orange sails which were hanging out to dry above the nested dories aboard three Portuguese motor fishing vessels which had entered harbour during the night. These two-thousand-ton ships had come in to take shelter from hurricane "Donna", which was recurving north from its sultry breeding ground off the West Indies. Though my stomach turned cold when I looked at the great white ships and realized what their presence in harbour implied, I knew that even leaving immediately, it would be October before I could hope to make my landfall, so I could not remain in this haven.

I could not bear to look at Fiona as I rolled down five feet of the mainsail, and at 3 p.m. G.M.T., hoisted sail, cast off and headed for the narrows. Only once did I glance back at the lonely figure standing on the pier. I dared not look again, so forlorn and fearful and doubly alone did I feel now. It was as if a light had been extinguished, leaving *Cardinal Vertue* and I to sail out through the gloom across a grey wilderness.

9

ORDEAL BY STORM

The glass is falling hour by hour, the glass will fall for ever,
But if you break the bloody glass you won't hold up the weather.
—LOUIS MACNEICE

WITH a fair wind *Cardinal Vertue* cleared St. John's narrows and headed north-east at four and a half knots. On this course we drew away from the land so slowly that it was nine hours before the last of the Americas, still clearly silhouetted against an orange sunset, dipped below the horizon.

That night the moon was full and it was brilliantly clear; it was cold and the sea choppy. At midnight a breaking crest splashed aboard but did no harm. I was lonely as never before; frightened and restless, so that I could neither rest nor sleep.

Our course was a great circle which curved from north-east to become east in latitude 60°, south of the Faroes. As we would still be crossing the Grand Banks for a day or so, I got out the *Newfoundland and Labrador Pilot*. I was struck by the unwonted poetic vein of one phrase: "In the interior (of Labrador) the only law is the immemorial code of lodge and hunting ground."

I was delighted, wondering when it was written, for the area in question contains some of the largest iron workings in the world!

By noon next day we had covered ninety-eight miles in the twenty-one hours since we left port. The large trawler *Santa Elvira* of Coruña passed close astern and I was cheered to observe that the seas were breaking across her 'tween decks, the water cascading out of her scuppers each time she rolled, while my decks were dry.

Towards evening I sighted the Norwegian trawler *Rindenes* of Florø, which stood towards me and hailed in English to ask whither I was bound. Neither he nor the Spaniard appeared to be heeding the hurricane warning. This at least was good to know. "I wish you fair winds," he called, resuming his course.

For some reason these simple words spoken by a grave, quiet man, put new heart into me. I felt included within a fellowship, and I warmed to this as a great honour, for the men of the distant trawler fleets form a noble brotherhood.

That night the fair northerly wind carried us clear of the Banks and next day there were no more trawlers. I reefed and unreefed, changed headsails and repaired the foreguy when it parted. The P.V.C. trousers which I had borrowed from Val had become so porous and leaky as to be useless. I wrote, with foreboding:

"Temperature 48°F. Got wet. Hands numb with cold—a foretaste?"

Everything on the ship reminded me of the mate's presence, and the loneliness did not seem to be abating. The nights were so long now; twelve full hours of darkness! I began to have disturbing dreams whose content varied but which always ended with a scene that would shock me awake, to lie trembling and sweating with fear until my racing heartbeats gradually slowed to normal.

In the dream we would be sailing towards a gaunt black crag surmounted by a deserted, unlit, lighthouse. The sea and sky would be those I had seen when I last looked out; usually a stormy cold sea, under driven cloud-wrack.

Why this dream should have recurred night after night, and what was the fear that it reflected, I do not know. There was no rock or lighthouse, lit or unlit, for fifteen hundred miles ahead; nor have I any recollection of having known this scene in real life. But every detail is so indelibly printed on my memory that I would recognize it at once should it ever be my lot to gaze upon it.

On our first full day at sea we had covered one hundred and fifteen miles, and by the following noon, September 8th, we had covered another hundred and nineteen miles and were passing five hundred miles south of Cape Farvel, the southernmost point of Greenland. But we would not be able to keep us this pace for much longer.

The WNW wind backed to SW and steadily increased. By two-thirty in the morning of September 9th, it had already reached force 7 and the glass was falling. At 4.30 a.m., when the wind was blowing forty miles per hour, gale force 8, I lowered the mainsail and ran on with the staysail sheeted hard in so that it should not flog.

By noon the wind had risen to forty-nine miles per hour, force 9, and the glass was still dropping.

"Pooped by a crest," I recorded, "but *Cardinal Vertue* is running well, steering by the vane. The seas are marching in all the grandeur of a full Atlantic gale now."

"12.30. Pooped again. Canvas dodger torn adrift."

The stout new canvas had split and every one of the brass eyes along the quarter to which it was laced had been sheared clean off.

At 1 p.m. the straining staysail sheet tore out the fairlead, which was screwed into the deck beams. The wind was now fifty miles an hour and I lowered all sail, and with sopping wet jeans clinging round my legs and water swirling round my ankles, steered before the gale. I was wet through and tired for I had not been able to sleep the night before because of the falling glass.

The seas grew larger and steeper now, until they began to curl over and break. Long lines of foam ran. Each time I saw a wave tilt slowly forward and collapse into frothy, snowy, beautiful, cotton wool I wondered if a yacht could withstand such a fearful impact. Soon a giant with toppling crest reared astern and came roaring down upon the ship, to burst over the quarter, pouring over me where I clung to the rail and sending the yacht spinning like a match box. Unscathed, she shook the sea from her deck, while I sat breathless and gasping, with water sloshing around my knees before it had time to drain away out of the cockpit.

I now did what I had read about, and streamed ninety feet of warp in a bight astern. This made the yacht almost unmanageable; she persistently ran with the seas abeam, only being held down-wind with the greatest difficulty. Even then she would repeatedly broach-to. Apart from hindering steering, the warp was ineffective as each large sea would sweep it forward until it lay coiled almost alongside. Whether a longer one would have proved more useful I do not know.

At 3.30 p.m. the wind was still south-west and still blowing at fifty miles an hour. I had been in the cockpit two and a half hours and was now too cold and tired to steer any more. So I put the helm down, set the vane, and hove-to on the starboard tack. The yacht lay well a-hull, tending to luff a little, though more than once she would be spun right round by a breaking wave.

The Calor gas cylinders were still firmly lashed down but the fastenings which had withstood five thousand miles of sailing were not adequate now. One cylinder was on its side, dented and rolling, hitting its neighbours and the sides of the bunks with terrific force. I screwed in more eyebolts and added extra lashings until it was secure. Then I tried to restore some order in the cabin, and pumped. For the second time that day water was up to the floorboards.

I wound the chronometer and stared out through the doghouse

window at the white seas and the streaming foam and spray, now mixed with fine rain, which howled across the sea's face obscuring the division between air and water. Sometimes a comber would sweep sideways across the wind. Above the waves, delicate storm petrels swooped through the grey rain. The glass continued to fall as I wedged myself into my bunk.

I was promptly shot out again as the ship was hurled onto her beam ends and the cabin momentarily engulfed in green darkness. It seemed incredible that wood, glass and metal could withstand such an impact, but *Cardinal Vertue* rode on as buoyantly as ever.

By 8 p.m. the wind had fallen to forty miles an hour, though the glass was still low and the rain had given way to fog. I took in the useless warp and re-rove the staysail sheet through a fairlead in a rope grommet which I had prepared. Then I cleared the spinnaker boom ready to boom out the staysail when the time should come to hoist. Turning to the pump I found that it was partially blocked and sticking, and that the water was again up to the floorboards.

At dusk the wind had dropped to force 7, but it still blew from the south-west and the glass had fallen a further point to 991 mb. I hoisted and boomed out the staysail then, and we went reeling away north-westward through the thinning mist, on the port gybe, making four knots. The glass stood persistently at 991, but it was good to be on our way again and I sang as we crashed and rolled through the night.

After midnight I slept a few hours, waking at 5 a.m. on September 9th to find that the wind had veered to the west-nor-west and we were sailing south-east. Bright moonlight and the glow of the Northern Lights threw the rigging into relief as I unboomed the staysail, gybed, and adjusted the vane.

An hour and a half later, when dawn broke clear and wild, the glass had risen a point but the wind had increased again to forty-one miles an hour, a force 8 gale out of the north-west. I pumped with great difficulty while the wind steadily increased in violence. By 9.30 a.m. it had reached force 9 again, forty-nine miles an hour, and a sea which burst over the quarter broached *Cardinal Vertue* to. I handed the staysail.

"It was just as well I did so," I wrote in the log later, "for as soon as it was down the wind began to blow harder than ever. Heavens, how hard it is blowing. While I was in the cockpit a sea broke over us, turning the ship right round. She seemed to be trying to fall off before the seas, so this time I hove-to a-hull with the helm loose and the vane set to steer her off the wind.

"Have spent the rest of the two hours since heaving-to pumping with the plunger pump in the cockpit and trying to clear the diaphragm pump. Will make coffee if I can manage it and have a try at sleeping. Glass 993–4 mb."

At 2 p.m., a great wave broke over the yacht, spinning her round again and sending books, charts and instruments flying. Water spurted through the thin crack between the washboards and the main hatch cover with such force as to soak everything in the cabin. Gybing round to heave-to on the port tack again and mopping-up operations occupied half an hour. *Cardinal Vertue* was tending to luff now, as she had done in the previous day's gale. I wondered whether the difference in her behaviour was due to the varying size and shape of the seas; there was a big cross sea running at this time.

The frontal clouds began to break up and patches of sunlight appeared. It seemed wrong to waste such an opportunity, so clinging on to the housed boom against the momentum of the ship's dizzy swoops and rolls, I tried to take some photographs. But though I shielded the camera from the spray as best I could I had not much hope for the result. Then I dismantled the pump and tried to clear it. The wind was down to forty-two miles an hour between the gusts.

I noted down at 2.30 p.m.: "Can't sleep, worse luck; too tense, I suppose; slight apprehensive feeling; motion too irregular to cook; lying in the bunk reading and eating dried fruit and sweets. I miss the mate very much and would rather be with her than here! This *is* interesting *and* exciting though! I have every hope, now the glass is rising after this morning's veer, that this will blow itself out soon and enable us to get going again without wasting more time with this lying a-hull nonsense!"

"8.30 p.m. There is a mackerel sky over low hurrying storm clouds, but the glass has risen to 1,002 mb and the wind has fallen to thirty-four miles an hour, but it is gusty and variable and the sea is still large.

"Have spent another hour clearing the diaphragm pump—mostly matches and hairpins! Partial success. Could not sleep this afternoon but rested. Will now have coffee, tinned fruit, bread and cheese; then hope to make sail.

"9.15 p.m. We are away at three knots on port gybe under sheeted staysail."

I had had only four hours sleep during the previous sixty-one hours.

But now that the glass was rising and the ship sailing once more, I could at last relax and I slept an unbroken eight hours. On waking, once I had shaken off the effect of my fear-dream of the unlit lighthouse on the crag, I felt wonderfully rested.

In the awesome swell left by the gale *Cardinal Vertue* rolled sickeningly, developing every few minutes an accelerating rhythmic roll which, at its crescendo, prevented me from doing anything except holding on.

After a further three-quarters of an hour the pump was finally cleared. It is a wonderful pump and this trouble had been my own fault for mounting it against the ship's frames without enough clearance.

Clothes, blankets, all my possessions, were wet. Yet I dared not open the main hatch as every now and then a dollop of water would plop aboard. In these conditions it was with some trepidation that I got out the sextant. What with the height of the seas, the rolling, the spray and the scurrying clouds which often hid the sun, the sight seemed likely to be a poor one. However, its accuracy was confirmed by two others later that afternoon.

In spite of two days when the wind had reached force 9, we had covered two hundred and sixty three miles since our last accurate noon position three days before.

The two gales had evidently been part of a single low-pressure system. The first from south-west with mist and rain and falling glass —typical warm front weather. The second, the nor'-wester, had shown all the cold front phenomena; a veer, rising glass and clearing sky.

Before evening the wind had dropped sufficiently for the genoa to be hoisted, and the rubber-sealed hatch in the cockpit, which gave access to the engine controls, could be safely opened. After some coaxing, the engine started and kept going hesitantly for half an hour. I was not to know when I switched it off that it had run for the last time. For after the drenching it was soon to receive it never started again, and on examination in port was found to be so corroded as to be good only for the scrap heap.

During the night the glass again began to fall. At one-thirty on September 11th the wind backed into the south-west and freshened, causing *Cardinal Vertue* to luff into the wind, her genoa flailing and vibrating. After I had handed it and lashed it down to the pulpit and stanchions, everything was secure and I could relax, to write at two-thirty:

"In spite of the falling glass and rising wind I know she is well snugged down, at any rate until gale force is reached. So I am being very rash and sleeping without boots, or (useless) P.V.C. trousers! Feet, legs and thighs damp for three days now, but at least they are warm in the blankets!

"7 a.m. No luck! Just at first light by the Greenwich time I am using *Cardinal Vertue* was thrown aback and hove herself to. Wind forty miles an hour, force 8. I set her on course again and pumped her dry. What a mercy the pump is still clear.

"At 8.30, a second fairlead was pulled out of the deck by the staysail sheet. The wind was now gusting to forty-six miles an hour."

I lowered the No. 1 staysail and tried to hoist the tiny 45-square foot No. 3 staysail whose sheets were already rove. But the power of that wind! As the sail filled the lee sheet parted and the minute sail took charge like some demented thing of enormous power. The clew made a blurred arc as it flew, and emitted a high pitched hum; the mast shook and rattled with the fearful force of the flogging; the weather sheet wrapped round everything in sight including my legs.

In the half hour that it took to make things fast the wind had risen to force 9 and I hove-to a-hull, with the vane set to head *Cardinal Vertue* up into the wind, as she was tending to luff this time rather than turn down wind.

I considered using the sea-anchor, but decided not to do so for the time being as the ship seemed to give way and slide easily before the breaking waves, and it seemed likely that a sea-anchor might hold her up to the pounding. I would try it only as a last resort.

The sea was combing all ways by this time. Not at all the stately procession of breathtaking rollers of the first gale on September 8th.

By midday the yacht was tending to fall off a little, instead of luffing as she had done earlier. Was this in spite of, or because of, the vane setting? I had to admit that with the irregular sea it was hard to tell how she *was* lying. She was riding easier than in the last two gales, but this meant little as the seas were so different.

"Perhaps the 19 mb the glass has dropped in fourteen and a half hours means that the warm front will soon be passing?" I speculated, and continued: "All my trousers are wet; have managed to make coffee and with this and the heavy black bread and jam, I feel better. At least I have nothing to complain of, after all I *did* challenge the winds by coming this way at this time of year, so now I must just learn to take it!"

The afternoon seemed endless. I made a stew, which was quite a triumph. I tried to read—anything that would take my attention from the sea outside. But neither the *Cave Paintings of France*, nor *Lolita*, nor the magazines given us by the mission launch, nor *Pilots*, nor even Dr. Hannes Lindeman's account of his two crossings of the Atlantic by canoe, could hold my attention for long.

The hiss of an oncoming breaker, its shattering blow as it hurled the ship on to her beam-ends and darkened the cabin, would be enough to distract my attention from anything. Usually reading of Lindeman's dreadful hardships cheered me up by making me feel that I was living in a palace in comparison; but this time I was beginning to feel really sorry for myself.

The wind, which had backed a little towards the south, continued to increase. By 4 p.m. it was blowing at fifty-eight miles an hour, force 10, and harder in the gusts. The shriek of the wind was frightening; the tops were blown off the waves and the whole sea became white.

"Thank God for these changes in the wind direction," I wrote. "They hold the seas down a little, for however frightful the force of the wind it is the waves that matter most.

"*Cardinal Vertue* tends to lie broadside or by the quarter, with a 10–20-degree list; but when hit by a sea she heels to 50 degrees. When will the wind veer and the glass rise, I wonder?

"I felt that I was getting demoralized down below and had better go out and face it. So I crawled about the deck, lashing down the sails more firmly, and took some photographs; doubting if they would survive the spray. I feel calmer since going on deck, but I am still scared."

I pumped again and waited, tense and uneasy. There seemed little I could do, and whatever I did might well be wrong for I had never known the like of this before.

It was *Cardinal Vertue*, not I, that was successfully riding out this gale. Proudly she accepted the challenge as, tossed to and fro like a cork, with reeling spars, she rode the waves. When a sea broke fair across her she would shudder to her oaken soul, then shaking herself free with cascades of water streaming from her decks, she would leap skyward once more, alive and free and whole.

The wind blew consistently at fifty-eight miles an hour up to around 6.30 p.m., when it began to ease a little and to veer towards the northwest. But the waves were still growing higher and steeper, and breaking with greater fury. Twice in fifteen minutes the yacht was hove over and buried by waves that sent us crashing and spinning into darkness, and which really frightened me. I dared not let her battle alone any longer. I must try to help.

So, at about 7 p.m., I took the helm and steered before the gale. We would climb dizzily up and up until the ship would be picked up by the crest and hurled forward. As she began to surf, with eight knots registering on the Smith's speed indicator, the water spouted high above the cockpit on each side, before curving over to fill it with a frothing mill-race of icy water, great sheets of which would be flung out over the stern as *Cardinal Vertue* lurched and bucked and threw her bow high as the crest left her.

It was wildly exhilarating but I was drenched to the skin to start

with, and after half an hour I was too chilled to continue. So at 7.30 I shackled the eye at the end of the sea-anchor warp to the wire strop round the transom, streamed it astern, and adjusted the vane to head the yacht down wind.

Twice big seas hit her, spinning her right round each time. The sea-anchor did not seem to be helping and *Cardinal Vertue* lay almost broadside on. But I was too tired to care. I was learning the aptness of the seamen's saying that when you are in a small boat in heavy weather, for every point the wind rises, your ship grows one foot smaller!

I pumped out the bilge as the water was now above the floorboards and exchanged my trousers for swimming trunks, because corduroys, slacks, jeans, pyjama trousers and underpants were all wet now. "Shades of New York and the Gulf Stream," I wrote. "This rig was more suitable then!"

16. The jury-rig with which *Cardinal Vertue* sailed back
to Plymouth after her dismasting.

17. *Cardinal Vertue* alongside at Mashford's Yard, Cremyll,
with only 12 feet of her 34-foot mast left standing.

18. (*Above*) New York and Third Man Home: *Cardinal Vertue*, in tow of a Coastguard cutter, heads for the Quarantine Station.

19. (*Left*) Blondie Hasler lends a hand on the author's arrival in New York. This cockpit view shows the speed-indicator on the doghouse bulkhead and, aft, the mass-balance of the self-steering gear.

The gale was rapidly blowing itself out now. As the last streaks of yellow stormy sunset faded from the sky, around 9.30, the wind had dropped to force 8 or 9. All lights aboard were fused.

At midnight, with the wind force 8, the glass rising steeply and the air temperature 48°F, I wrote by the light of the oil lamp in the cabin:

"As the pressure of the wind slackens, everything becomes lively. The sea is wildly lumpy now and the ship, no longer pressed down so much by the wind, leaps around like a jumping bean. I have pumped again and am now wearing a folded tartan blanket over my swim trunks, tied around my waist with a piece of rope—like some grotesque caricature of a Scotsman."

I should have made sail during the night, or at least taken in the sea-anchor. But I lay exhausted, and alternately shivered and slept until morning. Water was sloshing over the cabin sole again.

Without much difficulty I hauled in the sea anchor, only to find that the shackle had chafed the wire strop half-way through during the thirteen hours it had been in use, mostly after the gale had abated. Later it was discovered that a rim of paint had cracked all round the transom, where the terrific pull had threatened to wrench the stern bodily off—yet the sea-anchor had seemingly been ineffective in holding the ship stern-on to the seas.

I have since consulted the Daily Weather Reports of the British Meteorological Office. No ships were in my vicinity until September 11th, when a deep depression had formed not far to the north-west of me, and a front was passing. My position on the 11th was 52° 20′ N, 39° 50′ W, only one hundred and fifty miles west of Ocean Weather Ship C, which was at 52° 50′ N, 35° 30′ W.

At noon this weather ship reported a south-westerly gale of forty-two knots (force 9) and a mean wave height of fourteen feet. At noon the gale at my position had not yet veered, and I, too, was logging a south-westerly gale of force 9. By 6.0 p.m. the waves at the weather ship's position had reached a mean height of 17½ feet. The largest waves would be 40 per cent. bigger than this, some 24½ feet high.

The next two hours were occupied in disentangling the No. 3 staysail and its sheet, fitting a new fairlead, hoisting the No. 1 staysail, and pumping. It was a cold grey morning and swimming trunks beneath porous P.V.C. trousers offered little protection from the raw wind. The ship's motion was very severe.

I slept for a little while, then lit the stove to dry out the electric wiring and cook a leisurely meal, consisting of two eggs, toast, coffee and biscuits. Over breakfast I read Lindeman's book. What incredible courage he showed! During his second canoe crossing in 1956 he had no room to lie down for the first three weeks until some of his stores were eaten, and could only doze hunched up forward over his canvas spray deck. Twice he was capsized as he neared the West Indies. All he seemed to lack was a sense of humour and I, for one, could hardly blame him for that!

I listed the gale's damage:

A fairlead torn off the quarter and the cockpit coaming cracked by the sea-anchor strop; all lights still *caput*; ship leaking; damage to sea-anchor strop and foresail fairlead.

I concluded by writing, with feeling: "I am so thankful to have an intact boat, mast, rudder, wind vane, navigation equipment and food—My God, I am lucky!"

That grey day, September 12th, ended with the lights still not working. In the week since leaving St. John's we had covered five hundred and ninety-five miles. Our best day's run was one hundred and nineteen miles. We had only been on the wind for twenty-three hours, and had been hove-to in the three gales for a total of forty-two hours. On the debit side, the gales had made me so jittery that I could not take my eyes from the barometer, and consistently under-canvased the ship during the following week.

Though I had tried to be exact in my note-taking during the gales, in case the record should be of value, the strength and fury of the seas, the fearful din and the driving spray, made it hard to tell just what the wind, waves and ship were doing at any particular moment. I was so overawed that my "scientific detachment" failed to run to making some obvious observations, such as the period of the waves as we lay a-hull. Nevertheless, I found that even the attempt to be detached, and to describe everything that was happening, helped to replace fear by interest.

Even though I had become so nervous of the weather, the aching loneliness that I had felt after leaving St. John's had gone. This was my own familiar sea with which I felt content to be alone.

I was able to sleep for the whole of the next night, so that on September 13th, even though the sky was streaked with cirrus and the glass had fallen a little, I felt much better. After some more drying out, and by-passing a sodden fuse-box with a length of wire, I got the lights working once more. It was bitterly cold but the sun was shining on blue white-capped seas and a shark appeared and swam for a little while astern.

Life seemed to have returned to the sea again; the petrels were now joined by terns and gulls which wheeled around the ship.

But I was much less happy to sight two ships; for even though the lights were working again, with the engine dead the batteries could not be re-charged and I could not afford to leave navigation lights burning through twelve hours of darkness. But I drew some comfort from the thought that, unlike icebergs or the drifting logs I had seen off the St. Lawrence, ships did at least have radar. When fog closed in that afternoon I could only trust that they would use their radar scanners even more carefully during such thick weather.

At three-thirty the following morning I hoisted the genoa and realized with annoyance that the ship could well have carried it the previous day. How much time had I wasted? The sail had only been set an hour when, "A wind light as yet, but with strength in the gusts", caused me to lower it hastily, and write, "So here it is again, oh well!"

But I soon realized I was being unduly pessimistic, and to help combat the effects of nerves and laziness, I made the following resolution:

"Have decided in view of my recent reluctance to make sail that I will sleep without my warm blanket-kilt. This way I feel cold, so should sleep lighter. This afternoon my sleeping gear consisted of three Norwegian jerseys, swim trunks, safety-belt, ski socks and wellingtons!"

As darkness descended after a gloomy day of damp mist the sky cleared and for a long time I stood on the transom, holding on to the backstays, oblivious of the cold, feeling the lift and scend of the ship beneath me as she rolled her easting down beneath a cloudless sky.

Next day, September 15th, we ran another ninety miles before a force 5 breeze from the north-west. The ship was leaking much less now as her seams took up after the terrible pounding she had received.

The sun set in dubious orange splendour and the sky was still clear at 1 a.m. when the wake, and every breaking wave crest, were afire with cold phosphorescence. To the northward, cold greenish curtains of light soared upwards. It was a grand and awesome sight which was only marred for me by the unwelcome lights of a ship astern.

When I awoke on the morning of the 16th I found that the wind had backed east-of-south, and we were racing merrily away due northward.

While I was resetting the vane I saw a ship approaching and, hoisting the ensign and the flags M.I.K. (Please report me to Lloyds) which Val had lent me, altered course to intercept her. She was *Mathilda Thordein* of Uddevala and she flew an answering pennant in acknowledgment of my signal before continuing on her way.

I must be on the shipping lane between Belle Isle Strait, the northernmost entrance to the St. Lawrence, and Scandinavia. But as I had been unable to obtain longitude sights for two days I could not be certain. In any case there was nothing I could do about it.

The wind began to head us and for most of that day I set the

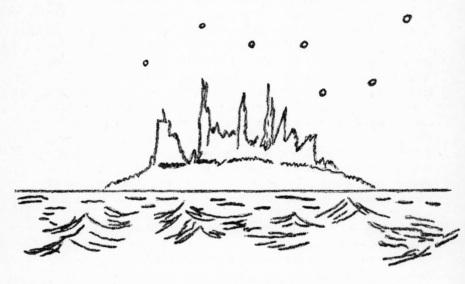

reefed mainsail. Then we sailed through varying winds, calms and rain squalls for the next one and a half days. My clothes and blankets began to dry and I even made pancakes, but not as well as the mate had done. We were now moving clear of the area 9–10 per cent. gales, which lay south of Greenland, and were entering a 7 per cent. gale region. Then there would be a square of 6 per cent. frequency until we had passed north of the prevailing westerlies, in latitude 60°, when we could expect finer weather.

These were busy days, occupied in taking sights, working for hours on the the silent engine, mending a split genoa and checking stores. With a spare battery aboard, I could afford to use the cabin lights if I was careful. This was just as well as paraffin was very short. All other stores were in good supply and I was certainly not losing weight this time.

All was going well; but the sea must never be taken for granted, lest the unexpected catch the unwary off-guard, as it nearly did me.

As I was hoisting the genoa one evening the wind gusted; and when the wind increases, things on the yacht behave quite differently. The usually docile genoa became wrapped about the forestay. The wire part of its halyard wound itself round the forestay the opposite way, while the halyard's rope tail, though cleated, still had enough play to loop over a spreader.

While I was disentangling the muddle the ship gave a violent lurch which pitched me neatly off the lee bow. I was not using the safety-belt but I clutched the wire guard rail as I passed, locking my arms and legs so firmly about it that I was a minute in freeing myself and clambering back aboard. Though the danger was over in under a second the incident left me thoroughly shaken.

In the early morning hours of September 18th, a new gale began to blow out of the north-west. The aurora swept across the northern sky and upwards from east and west to arch, blazing, across the zenith. Between rain squalls, the lights flickered until dawn behind ragged black cloud masses. The wind cut like a knife—as well it might, blowing as it did straight off the Greenland ice cap, five hundred and fifty miles away.

Though the wind was blowing at forty miles an hour I managed, in spite of the wild motion, to boil an egg and laid it down tenderly, wrapped in a cloth. When I turned back to it a moment later it had plastered itself against *both* sides of the cabin! How it did it is a mystery.

At 10 a.m., between the sheets of spray and rain squalls, I managed to obtain a sight of the sun. The log entry: "Calor gas cylinder changed at 2.30 p.m." covers a good deal of effort. Doing anything at all in a gale is unbelievably difficult. I was boiling salt fish and doing my best to stop the water from splashing out of the saucepan, and shampooing my hair at the same time, when the gas ran out. While I was wrestling with the cylinder's locking nut, we broached-to. When the ship had been set back on course, the sheets needed attention. Then the ties on the furled mainsail had to be reinforced; and an opportunity had to be taken to obtain a sight. After all this I could return to the cylinder.

By the time the fresh one was in place the gale was howling at forty-eight miles an hour, and a sea, bursting over the quarter, spun us round and broached us to, this time aback. I noted that "The effect of the breaking waves seems to depend on whether they hit the ship forward, or aft, or a-beam. According to where the weight of the blow falls, the yacht spins round accordingly or is thrown bodily sideways. Exactly the same seems to happen whether she is running, or hove-to in some fashion."

The gale died down during the night. For the first time we had not had to heave-to but had been able to keep running under reefed No. 1 staysail.

How stiff the gales had left me! Not bruised so much, because by now I was pretty canny at hanging on, but aching in every joint through being thrown about like a dice in a cup.

The next day, September 19th, was the end of the second week out. The wind had been mainly fair, in fact the mainsail had only been hoisted for eleven and a half hours. We had covered five hundred and ninety-four miles. The best day's run was one hundred and twenty miles.

That night the wind backed to east-of-south and a rapidly falling glass foretold further trouble. I hoisted the mainsail at 4.30 a.m. when the wind was south-east and we could still lay our course. By 5.30 the genoa had to be handed as the wind, which had backed further to east-south-east, was increasing.

Two hours later I awoke to a strong smell of Calor gas, but had no time to investigate as the ship was hard pressed. As I was rolling down the mainsail the topping lift jammed between the boom and its clew fitting and locked solid. Eventually, with a turn of the sheet, I was able to restrain the wildly threshing boom, which jerked me to and fro until my teeth rattled, for long enough to enable me to cut the nylon cord with which I had replaced the topping lift shackle.

When I had captured and made fast the topping lift again it was time to reef the staysail. As I set the ship at the short steep head seas which the force 6 breeze had raised, spray and rain drove over us until I was soaked through my inadequate P.V.C.'s.

Now that I at last had leisure to look for the Calor leak I found that I must have kicked open the valve of an almost empty cylinder in the dark. I did not know if a dangerous amount of gas had escaped, so to be on the safe side I aired the ship at the cost of a good deal of water down the fore hatch.

At 11 a.m. with the wind up to force 7, I close-reefed the mainsail and raised the gallows to allow the boom to set lower, beneath it. The sheet could not function in this position so I lashed the boom down to a cleat. The sail set flatter this way, without flogging, and *Cardinal Vertue* punched her way to windward into the stinging rain at four knots. "It is back to swimming trunks again, I am afraid," I wrote. "Thank goodness I had the foresight to fry an egg at 4 a.m."

By 1 p.m. the wind had reached forty-two miles an hour and the glass was still steadily falling. Two hours later it was blowing forty-five miles an hour and we were continuing to make headway to windward.

But when the wind, blowing persistently from the east-south-east, increased to fifty miles an hour, force 9, at 5 p.m., I hove-to on the starboard tack under the close-reefed mainsail by lowering the staysail and lashing the helm down with the tiller lines.

I thought we had been able to keep going for so long because the gale had come up at right angles to the prevailing westerly Atlantic swell. Now the yacht rode comfortably hove-to.

It was hard to visualize what life would be like without the wind-vane. I became chilled, wet and exhausted after only half an hour on deck or in the cockpit in bad weather; I could never have steered for hour after hour in these conditions.

The wind eased during the evening but it was a foul night with rain squalls, a fearsome cross sea, a falling glass and a wind that neither veered nor backed. What did such weather mean? Was the "low" north or south of us, or where?

Whatever the signs portended, the wind continued to ease until I could no longer in decency remain hove-to; so before midnight I crawled out of my warm bunk and got under way. This was only a matter of hoisting the staysail, freeing the helm and unrolling some of the mainsail. I would have been more reluctant to get under way had there been warps or a sea-anchor to get aboard.

"How easily I could have gone to sleep and missed this opportunity to press on if I had allowed myself to be hypnotized by the falling glass!" I wrote smugly. "Why it is as smooth as a pond outside—or almost!"

I turned over and went to sleep with the wind east-south-east and light, and woke at 2 a.m. to find it blowing a force 8 gale again from the north-west, almost exactly the opposite quarter.

After I had lowered the mainsail and resumed the proper course under reefed staysail, I noted in a more chastened mood, "So *now* I know what the unchanged wind direction, with steadily falling glass followed by a lull, meant. I should have guessed, of course, that the centre of a depression was passing clean over us. But no! the 'clever' navigator had to go to sleep about 1 a.m. and only wake when his ship was luffing hard and sailing in the wrong direction!" This was later confirmed from the Daily Weather Reports of the British Meteorological Office.

The wind continued to blow at forty-one miles an hour between squalls. Twice before daybreak *Cardinal Vertue* had broached-to and been thrown a-back. At 11.30 a.m. the gale was still blowing at forty miles an hour but the glass had begun to rise and the sunshine to break through. I climbed on to the housed boom and up the mast a little way to try to get level with the tops of the waves in order to judge their height more accurately than I could from the cockpit, from where they had seemed enormous. To my chagrin I found that they were much lower than I had expected, only about 14 feet high on average!

According to Cdr. Errol Bruce in *Deep Sea Sailing*, a force 8 gale of unlimited fetch and starting from a calm would raise a sea 12½ feet high in nine hours. On September 21st the north-west gale had been blowing at force 8 for nine hours when I made my observation of wave height, but it had not blown from a calm. It had followed, after a three-hour lull, a nine-hour east-south-easterly gale which had reached force 9 for several hours.

On the other hand, the fetch was not unlimited. According to the Daily Weather Reports the distance from the centre of the disturbance which caused the gale was less than two hundred miles. This distance, and not that from the nearest land to windward, determines the fetch, and therefore the height, of the waves.

At noon, an hour after my note, a ship to the north of me was still experiencing gale-force winds, but I was only logging force 7. Ocean Weather Ship I, in 59° N, 19° W, which was some ninety miles north-east of me (my position was 58° 08′ N, 20° 24′ W) also recorded a wind which had fallen from force 8 to force 7 (28 knots), and confused waves 13 feet high. My own estimate of 14 feet as the height of the seas would therefore be about correct.

The wind moderated during the day and that night I was able to lie in my bunk looking through the doghouse windows at the Northern Lights, which, between hail storms, illumined the inky thunder clouds with unearthly magnificence, and listening to Paul Robeson singing negro spirituals on Radio Luxembourg. His magnificent voice formed a fitting counterpart to those remote glowing curtains which hung at the edge of space, high over Iceland, three hundred miles to the north.

The next day was notable for the discovery of two packets of mildewed bacon I had overlooked. As it would not keep much longer, I cooked it all and dined sumptuously on bacon, eggs, fried bread and coffee.

On the radio's trawler band I could now hear the fishermen talking to each other from the Outer Bailey or Lousy Banks. How had these banks come by their name, I wondered, and I sighed for a moment at the memory of the Grand Banks, now so far astern.

Ships passed by nearly every day now; far too many for comfort. They were bound to or from Canada, via Pentland Firth, or between the Faroes and the Shetland Isles.

While I had good reason to be concerned about steamers, my other fear was quite irrational. This was of hitting Rockall. This isolated rock spire rises 70 sheer feet out of the depths some one hundred and sixty miles west of St. Kilda in the Hebrides. Over the centuries it had often been sighted but it was not until 1810 that its existence was finally established by H.M.S. *Endymion*. Prior to this time it had often been taken for a full-rigged ship under sail, so steep was it and so white with bird droppings. On one side of the rock dangerous reefs extend for some miles. In New York I had marked these on a chart from the information in Blondie Hasler's *North Atlantic Pilot*. Now I found that I had left this particular chart behind and could not remember on which side of Rockall the reefs lay. But I had nothing to worry about because I had obtained good sights which showed that when I passed Rockall next day I would be sixty miles north of it.

During the morning of September 23rd the weather again deteriorated. The wind backed to the south-east and began to rise; while the sea became shrouded by a dismal fine rain. The high-tension battery of the radio took this opportunity to give out and I found to my dismay that one of the leads of the spare battery had corroded. The delicate work of "pirating" a lead from the used battery was difficult in such a seaway, so that I was surprised and delighted to get the set working. Any day now the B.B.C. time signals should become audible, when I could correct any error in the deck-watch. I had no wish to impale the ship on any of the fearsome Gaelic rocks like Sula Sgeir, whose jagged spires guard the northern Hebrides.

For three hours after the wind had reached forty miles an hour we beat to windward into the driving rain and spray under close-reefed main and reefed staysail.

At 5 p.m. the wind veered to south-east which allowed me to run before the gale. Slipping out of my kilt, I went on deck wearing a hooded P.V.C. smock and three pullovers but with nothing below but my swimming trunks and knobbly knees, purple with cold and goose pimples. It was as well I handed the mainsail when I did for a few minutes later the wind was shrieking at forty-eight miles an hour and *Cardinal Vertue* was running at five knots under reefed staysail alone. Fortunately the sea was confused and relatively small, as yet.

Every now and then the yacht would broach-to or be thrown a-back, so I kept wearing my P.V.C. smock in the cabin, ready to climb out of the hatchway in a hurry and set the yacht back on course; for this time I was determined to keep going if possible.

Between 6.30 and 8 p.m., the wind blew at fifty-three miles an hour and *Cardinal Vertue* tended to luff and run across the seas; the action of her vane repeatedly overpowered by blows from the steep, breaking crests. I steered for half an hour before seas which seemed mountainous to me. The Smith's indicator registered nine and a half knots when we surfed and the cockpit was filled with swirling water. Even though my safety-belt was in use I would grasp the guard rail and hang on whenever a wave steeper and higher than the rest climbed toppling above the stern before cascading over me.

Once, while I was out on the transom adjusting the wind-vane, a sea burst across us, broaching us to. The water swirled around my knees as I struggled for foothold on the after deck, while over my shoulder all that I could see of the ship was her doghouse, part of the weather rail, and the mast.

This was enough steering for me; darkness was falling and the surface of the sea was being blown into white smoke. I retired below and hoped that the vane could carry on.

"I don't know how much longer she can keep going," I wrote doubtfully, then continued wistfully, "The mate would have looked far more becoming than me, dressed like this! Come to think of it, I wish the mate were here!" Then with something less than gallantry, I coupled the last sentiment with: "I wish I had some whisky, too! and I wish the wind would ease; I am being bounced all over the cabin."

I was lucky indeed, for by nine-thirty, the wind had fallen to force 8 and less heavy water was coming aboard. This was the sixth gale; but this time we had made it without having to heave-to at all.

It was true that I had also successfully kept going through the gale on September 18th but it had been a milder one, the wind velocity only exceeding force 8 for a short period.

According to the Daily Weather Reports a "low" had passed over my position on the afternoon of the 23rd. No ships were in my vicinity or near its centre, but the following day a vessel in its track reported winds of forty-seven knots, force 9.

What had been the height of the waves which I had described as "mountainous"? As the disturbance passed clear of Ocean Weather Ship I, no data is available. I would judge the waves to be about the same as those on September 11th, which were recorded by Weather Ship C as having a mean height of 17½ feet, so occasional very large seas might have reached 24½ feet, but such waves would be rare.

The next day I was irritable and drained of energy as always after a gale. Every joint ached where it had been jerked and snapped to and fro. Souvenirs of the gale were everywhere; an overturned saucepan of stew in the food locker, pools of water in incredible places, a violent motion which lingered on in the swell, without the thumps and thundering cascades but also without the inimitable grandeur of the storm.

On consulting the tables, after taking a sight, I found that the sun had now crossed the Equator into southerly declination, abandoning us to the northern winter. We were crossing longitude 10° W, that is, we were passing the extreme tip of Ireland, four hundred and twenty miles south of us. That night, beneath the remote aurora, I obtained the first B.B.C. time signal.

The wind now became fickle and capricious. The reason for this was that the European wind systems were cushioning the Atlantic gales, in particular the westerlies were dissipated against a stable anticyclone which was sitting firmly on the Norwegian Sea.

By morning, the wind was blowing steadily from eastward, dead ahead, and for the next three days we plunged and bucked to windward on the starboard tack.

On the second day I was sighted and reported by the Swedish ship *Ragneberg*, and a few hours later I caught a glimpse of a submarine's conning-tower between the waves.

Next morning the stainless steel lee runner frayed through and had to be joined with bulldog grips and supported by a tackle.

When I reached the latitude of the Faroes, and was north of Shetland altogether, in 61° 13′ N, I could at last lay Sumburgh Head on the other tack. I came about and sailed south-east through a day of sunshine and a night during which a great black cloud hung over us to port like a cliff, silhouetted first against the aurora, then the dawn. At daybreak a few scattered clouds lay on the eastern horizon but as the sun rose higher on September 29th they scattered—all but one!

"This bloody maritime weeping act is trying to start again!" I wrote, with disgust, in the log. But it was no cloud that lay ahead, it was Foula, first island of Shetland, its cliffs rising sheer, 1,200 feet out of the sea.

The wind died and for the next twenty-three and a half hours I lay becalmed, watching the unchanging shape of Foula, which some say was the "Ultima Thule" of the Romans. The stove was giving up now but would still cook slowly. Though I was able to dry out properly for

almost the first time in three weeks, I still knew little peace of mind until the wind gave the ship life next morning, September 30th, heeling her over on the port tack. "After this long unexpected calm in sight of land," I wrote, "I feel as if my free-will had been 'wrung-out'. Far more than a gale, a calm brings home our smallness before nature."

All day Foula grew larger, until by 4 p.m. West Hoevdi Cliff stood gigantic above the ship. One by one the hills of the Shetland mainland rose out of the sea ahead; hosts of seabirds dotted the water, a dolphin appeared, then a seal.

Through light airs and brief calms I stood on as night fell, revealing the lights of trawlers scattered over the sea. "A wonderful day with some progress and above all some feeling of self-mastery over the effects of what I find hardest to bear—calms," I wrote. "Now the cliffs of Hoevdi are tinged with rose. One feels a special quality in these Norse Isles, as if the old gods still linger here."

At midnight I tried to describe the scene: "The moon stands high to the right, and a most brilliant aurora arches over the sky on the left. Around us is a vast panorama of islands; Foula astern now, Fair Isle to the southward and Sumburgh Head silhouetted against the stars on the port bow with its lighthouse blinking. Ahead, too, lies Sumburgh Röst. Now the wind is falling light again and heading us as we sail on into the October night."

I felt great thankfulness at having passed safely through my ordeal by storm, but as I gazed out at the vastness around me, I wrote, "I wonder when next I shall see its like again?"

Wilfred Noyce in *Springs of Adventure* has expressed my feelings far better than I:

> Who has known heights and depths shall not again
> Know peace—not as the calm heart knows
> Low ivied walls, a garden close,
> The old enchantment of a rose,
> And though he tread the humble ways of men
> He shall not speak the common tongue again.

10

SHETLAND LANDFALL

"This dangerous race in which the sea runs to great heights, and breaks with violence, at times even in calm weather extends . . . two to four miles off Sumburgh Head. . . . As in this confused tumbling and bursting sea, vessels often become completely unmanageable and sometimes founder, while others have been tossed about for days together in light weather, the röst should be given a wide berth."

Sumburgh Head Röst—
North Sea Pilot, Part One (1910 Edition)

EVEN though I had no such detailed account as this of the röst on board, I aimed to keep well clear of a place with such an evil reputation. As long ago as A.D. 81, Agricola's Roman fleet "discovered and subdued islands hitherto unknown, which they call the Orkneys. Thule too was seen . . . but they reported that the sea was *sticky and heavy for the rowers.*" This seems a good description of the röst.

Then the Orkneyingers' Saga tells how "Earl Erlend and Sweyn held on south at once into the Isles with five ships and got caught in Dynrace (Sumburgh Röst) in dangerous tides and a storm of wind, and there they parted company. Then Sweyn bore up for Fair Isle with two ships and they thought the Earl lost. Then they held on their course under Sanday and there Earl Erlend lay before them with three ships and that was a very joyful meeting."

I had planned to keep a good offing from Sumburgh Head but the wind veered and headed me, so that the best course I could lay led right through the middle of the röst, barely clearing the headland itself.

But the tide would only remain favourable until 7 a.m. so that if I tacked away southward I could not hope to round the Cape in the face of light contrary winds and a foul tide until some time in the afternoon. Furthermore, when the tide changed it set southwards, away from the land for the first few hours, so if there were any bother in the race *Cardinal Vertue* would soon be swept clear.

Nevertheless, I closed the röst with some care and trepidation, writing in the log: "Even the Saga tells of a Viking fleet caught here in a gale; this is no gale; but I am no Viking either!"

Over the stern the aurora still stood like an archway leading from a faery land that we were leaving, as at 5.30 a.m. on October 1st we entered Sumburgh Röst and for nearly two hours were tossed and shaken until I felt sick and giddy. Great pyramids of water would hump up, erupt and topple; a frightening sight, even in that light easterly weather.

In the midst of this wild ride we came upon a sleeping seal lying on his back and twitching his grey whiskers irritably whenever a wave splashed him. He looked for all the world like some old gentleman dozing in a club armchair. An expression of comical alarm spread over his face when he opened his eyes and saw the ship beside him; then he flipped over and dived in a flash of sleek dark grace.

The clouds were pink and orange in the sunrise as we rounded the ness and sailed into calmer water, bearing away for Bressay Sound.

With a fair breeze, *Cardinal Vertue* ran swiftly up the coast of Shetland. By 10.15 we were passing the Pictish Broch on Mousa Island, a round tower, relic of a vanished race, which has provided a prominent sea mark since the first Norse invaders "fed the ravens with the harvest of their spear-storms".

It was 12.35 p.m. when we entered Lerwick Harbour and rounded-to alongside Tom Moncrief's schooner *Loki*; while a Shetland model sailed by like some miniature longship.

St. John's lay one thousand nine hundred and eighty-four miles, and twenty-five days twenty-one hours, astern. For two-thirds of the way we had run before the wind, usually without a mainsail but we had not been off the wind during the past five days. There had been five force 9 gales and one which reached force 10.

I seemed in a daze that afternoon and my impressions are hazy. I remember handing back a battered sextant, and finding kindness and hospitality that I can never forget. I recall Basil Wishart in the newspaper office asking me who had sailed that way before. I did not know; so he took up the telephone. When he replaced the receiver he turned to me, grinning:

"He says, 'No one since Leif Erikson!'"

Tom suggested that I should be broken-in to the land gently by way of a cruise into the Voes aboard *Loki*. As we clambered aboard, his son remarked: "Dad didn't expect you."

"Why not?" I asked puzzled. "Didn't he get the card I sent him from St. John's?"

"We got it all right, that's *why* he didn't expect you. When he read your card he said: 'That's the last we've seen of him!' "

As the stately 27-tonner breasted the swells beyond the Sound, I stood alone in the dusk remembering Shelley's lines:

> The wilderness has a mysterious tongue
> Which teaches awful doubt, or faith so mild,
> So solemn, so serene, that man may be,
> But for such faith, with nature reconciled.

For a little while I had been living intimately with things greater than myself. Tom was right in saying that I needed time to become fully part of the civilized world again, for I knew that I had been subtly changed, a man of deeper calm and confidence perhaps, but above all, imbued with profound humility.

THIS BOOK IS DEDICATED TO

FIONA, MY WIFE

20. Fiona, with David Lewis and Blondie Hasler, aboard *Cardinal Vertue*.

21. H.R.H. the Duke of Edinburgh presents the author with his award. On the right is Lt.-Col. Odling Smee, Rear-Commodore of the Royal Western Yacht Club, the organizers of the race.

APPENDIX ONE

Cardinal Vertue

Cardinal Vertue is a Vertue-class Bermudan sloop, designed by J. Laurent Giles and built by E. F. Elkins and Co. at Christchurch in 1948. Her port of registry is London and her official number is 183341. Principal dimensions are:

Length, overall	..	25 ft. 3 in.
Length, waterline	..	21 ft. 6 in.
Beam	..	7 ft. 2 in.
Draft	..	4 ft. 6 in.
Displacement	..	4.5 tons
Thames measurement	..	5 tons

Sail areas

Mainsail	..	180 sq. ft.
Genoa	..	230 sq. ft.
Spinnaker	..	400 sq. ft. approx.
No. 1 staysail	..	98 sq. ft.
No. 2 staysail	..	68 sq. ft.
(or No. 1 reefed)		
No. 3 staysail	..	45 sq. ft.

Modifications made for the Race

An inner lining of five-ply was fitted to the side of the doghouse between the windows. This was to prevent the mahogany splitting along the grain in the event of a knockdown.

The Triplex windows were covered outside with Perspex, and brass strips backed the grooves in which the washboards slide down. Originally only ¼ in. of wood held the washboards in position, and they would have been vulnerable to a bursting sea from astern.

Hand-rails were fitted inside the cabin and proved invaluable.

A diaphragm pump (Mike Henderson) was fitted beneath the cabin floorboards. It was most efficient and would have been unblockable except that I mounted it too low. Far superior, in my experience, to plunger and semi-rotary pumps.

A canvas dodger surrounded the cockpit.

Non-slip decks were obtained by sprinkling a wet undercoat with silver sand, brushing off the surplus when dry, and covering with a top coat.

The fore-hatch was bedded on rubber strips, fitted with a hasp and also lashed down, all from inside. It proved watertight.

Heavy insulated cable was used throughout for electric wiring.

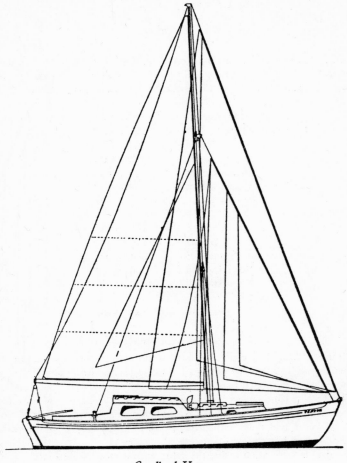

Cardinal Vertue

The self-draining cockpit was reduced in size to standard Vertue s-d. dimensions and two $1\frac{1}{2}$-in. drains fitted. Two-inch drains would have been better. Locker tops were bedded down on rubber strips and fastened with hasps.

Mainsail and twin No. 1 staysails of 10-oz. Terylene were made specially

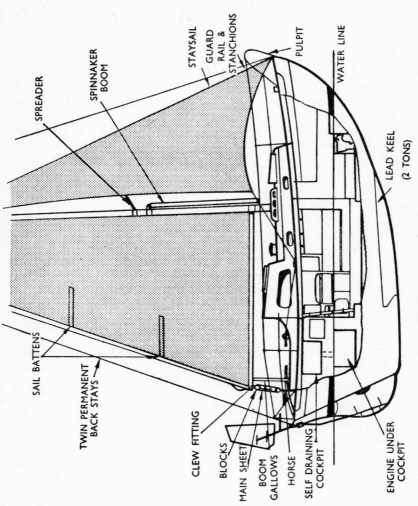

SPREADER

SPINNAKER
BOOM

STAYSAIL

GUARD
RAIL &
STANCHIONS

PULPIT

WATER LINE

LEAD KEEL
(2 TONS)

SAIL BATTENS

TWIN PERMANENT
BACK STAYS

CLEW FITTING

BLOCKS

MAIN SHEET

BOOM
GALLOWS

HORSE

SELF DRAINING
COCKPIT

ENGINE UNDER
COCKPIT

Cardinal Vertue: elevation.

for the race by Gowens of West Mersea. Though they flogged violently at times there was no damage and only one small area of chafe where the topping lift touched the lower part of the leach of the mainsail. If I had not been so secretive about where I was going, Gowens would have fitted shackles for the slides. These would have been better than seizing. The staysail was fitted with reef points at Humphrey Barton's suggestion and this proved a great success.

The main boom was shortened and twin masthead backstays fitted (alternative Vertue pattern). *Cardinal Vertue* is as fast with her new smaller mainsail as with her larger cotton one.

A main boom foreguy was fitted on the recommendation of Humphrey Barton. It holds the boom down and safe from an unexpected gybe, yet can be quickly released. The disadvantages, which to my mind are quite outweighed by its advantages, are: (i) strain on stanchions, as the foreguy must pass outside everything; (ii) the foreguy easily chafes through.

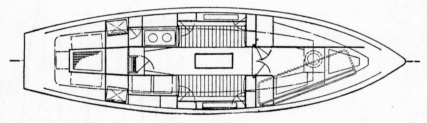

Cardinal Vertue: plan.

The rigging was of stainless steel but I was in error in using too small a block round which the running part of the lee runner had to pass. With a bigger block it would not have been bent at such an acute angle and would not have chafed through.

P.V.C. covering was carried well up shrouds and over the guardrail. There was no chafe of sails or sheets and baggy-wrinkle was never needed.

A permanent gallows was already fitted.

A permanent topping-lift, kept taut by a length of shock cord, had been fitted and I replaced the shackle by a length of nylon cord to facilitate lengthening the topping-lift as the boom dropped lower when close-reefed.

Some Notes on Equipment

Radio D.F. set: I made the mistake of mounting mine too near the hatchway where it was damaged by spray. A model whose loop is mounted on a hand-bearing compass is easier to use when alone, as you cannot take a radio bearing and read the direction the ship is heading on the steering compass at the same time.

Safety-belt: The most useful piece of equipment of all.

Inflatable covered rubber dinghy: The ideal one for the ocean cruiser has not yet been made. Should disaster overtake a yacht on an ocean crossing no one would know anything was wrong for months and even then would

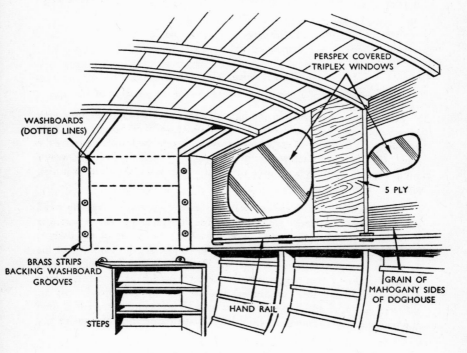

Cardinal Vertue: cabin details.

not know where to look. Ideally, therefore, an ocean-going yacht's emergency rubber dinghy should be capable of sailing into the nearest shipping lane, i.e. it should be oval and have a sail and either a keel or lee-boards.

Echo-sounder: A transistor set is an invaluable navigational aid when in soundings.

Sextant: A micrometer type is far easier to read than one with a vernier. I shall try to borrow one again next time I go to sea.

Navigation: I used Lt. Cdr. Rantzen's book together with the *Abridged Nautical Almanac* and H.D.486. I needed three volumes of these tables to cover from New York to Lerwick. H225A, the sight form for use with these tables, simplifies navigation enormously by listing each step in the process of working a sight, so ensuring that none is missed.

Insurance: The underwriter was most reasonable. Insurance for twelve months, seven in commission including the two-way Atlantic crossing, on a value of £1,800, was the same as for an earlier voyage to Norway, namely:

$$£36 \ 3s. \ 0d.$$

Third party   1   5s.   0d.
Racing cover   6   0s.   0d.

Total premium £43   8s.   0d.

An excess clause of £100 was in operation for the duration of the race.

Unnecessary equipment: In the light of experience I found the following items to have been unnecessary: (i) Twin spinnaker booms and twin running sails (twin No. 1 staysails)—these were rendered superfluous by the vane; (ii) Sea-anchor and sea-anchor strop; (iii) Tackle for hoisting oneself up in bosun's chair. When I used the chair, it was less effort to hoist it first, then climb up into it.

Desirable additional equipment and precautions include: (i) Non-slip tread on the companion ladder steps and on the cockpit seats; (ii) A stronger gooseneck; (iii) A better spray hood than the present one of my design; (iv) Tapered slats glued along the boom to counteract the tendency of the boom to droop when close-reefed; (v) Better protection of engine from damp; (vi) For a long trip a paraffin cooker would have been better than Calor gas (though less convenient) because bottled gas threads vary in different countries and heavy cylinders have to be carried (surely it is time the manufacturers came to an international standardization agreement!).

APPENDIX TWO

The Self-steering Gear on "Cardinal Vertue"

Cardinal Vertue's self-steering gear was of the trim-tab or servo-rudder type. The design was my own but was based on the advice and experience of others, especially Val Howells. It was made by the brothers Foster of The

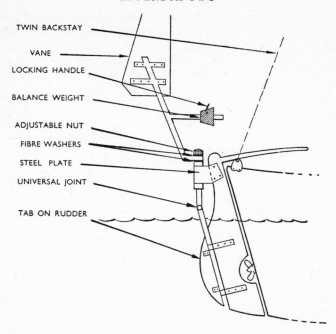

TWIN BACKSTAY

VANE

LOCKING HANDLE

BALANCE WEIGHT

ADJUSTABLE NUT

FIBRE WASHERS

STEEL PLATE

UNIVERSAL JOINT

TAB ON RUDDER

Aries Engineering Company of East Ham, and by Jack Staines of Tucker Brown and Co. of Burnham-on-Crouch, who made the trim-tab.

In operation the ship is set on course and the sheets correctly trimmed. The vane is allowed to trail with the wind and is then locked to connect it to the tab. If the ship moves off course to port, as shown in the diagram overleaf, the wind strikes the right-hand side of the vane, pushing it over to port. This moves the trim-tab to port, too. The water pressure against the trim-tab forces the main rudder to starboard, and the ship, turning to starboard, resumes her course.

The vane itself was made of marine five-ply and was probably unnecessarily heavy. The tab, too, was rather too large in proportion to the wetted surface of the rudder. During trials, a tremendous vibration would develop at certain angles of tab, due apparently to cavitation. This was cured, on the advice of Mike Henderson, by thinning down the tab.

It is essential that the device be as free from friction and as well-balanced as possible. The two ball-races on which the shaft turns are lubricated by a grease nipple and were most satisfactory. The universal joint is of stainless steel and kept freely mobile.

In the light of experience I would now make the following improvements to the gear.

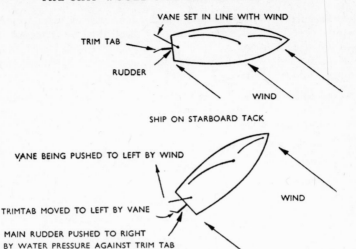

If the ship moves off course to port as shown in the diagram above, the wind strikes the right-hand side of the vane pushing it over to port. This moves the trim-tab to port too. The water pressure against the trim-tab forces the main rudder to starboard; the ship, turning to starboard, resumes her course.

(i) A light vane for gentle winds. My gear, like Val Howells', did not work properly in force 1–2 breezes. I had to steer by hand under 2½ knots, as rudder and vane would be thrown over by the swell and the ship be taken a-back when winds were very light.

(ii) An inboard control in cockpit or cabin, as was successfully used aboard *Jester*.

(iii) A calibrated indicator so that the vane could be set at marked positions.

(iv) A slightly smaller trim-tab and vane.

(v) A wheel locking-nut which would be more convenient than the short handle I used.

Setting the vane: In a normal craft with some weather helm, the vane is not set exactly down wind but with a few degrees bias one way to counteract the weather helm. I can never remember the direction of this bias but, like its amount, it is soon found by trial and error.

Effect of quartering seas: As described in Chapter 6, each quartering sea slews the yacht round, after which she swings back on course by the action of the vane. If, however, the seas are steep, this constant driving of the ship off course can produce a zigzag well to windward of the course required. Val

Howells experienced the same trouble, and in both cases our ships maintained their correct courses when the mainsail was lowered and we proceeded under genoa or staysails alone.

Vane steering for other craft: Counter sterns and bumpkins present problems which may be tackled in various ways.

(i) Leaving the main rudder free, the vane can be attached to an auxiliary rudder fitted to the counter. A reverse linkage must be incorporated here. (*See Mike Henderson's article on "Mick the Miller" in* Yachting World, *April 1957 and "Jean Matilde's Gear"*, Yachting Monthly, *June 1959.*)

(ii) A large vane can be made to work the main rudder direct, again through a reverse linkage, as successfully used by Francis Chichester.

(iii) For a counter-stern yacht a trim-tab can be used if there is room to run a shaft down the rudder trunk and connect it to the tab by side arms. Ian Major used this method on *Buttercup*.

Other methods of self-steering: Hamilton used a boomed-out genoa connected to the tiller by its sheet, the tiller being held under tension by shock-absorber cord. The Hiscocks in *Voyaging under Sail* describe various twin headsail layouts but the ever-changing winds of our latitudes make such systems cumbersome for other than trade-wind passages. They do not confer on the single-hander that "freedom of the ocean" which goes with the ability to make self-steered passages through the variables. Whatever the method employed, a balanced hull and sail plan are desirable if a yacht is to steer herself efficiently.

APPENDIX THREE

The Race and the Competitors

The First Single-handed Transatlantic Race from Plymouth to New York, originally suggested by Lt.-Col. H. G. Hasler, was organized by the Royal Western Yacht Club of England, with the Slocum Society responsible for the finishing arrangements. The object of the race was to encourage the development of suitable boats, gear, supplies and techniques for single-handed ocean crossings under sail. Yachts of any size or type were eligible but no means of propulsion could be employed other than the force of the wind, the manpower of the crew, or both. A competitor, to qualify, must have completed a single-handed cruise of a nature to satisfy the organizing committee or produce a certificate of competence endorsed by a recognized yacht club.

The start of the race was from Plymouth at 10.0 a.m. B.S.T. on June 11th, 1960. Competitors could proceed by any route to the finishing line off the Ambrose light-vessel in the approaches to New York harbour and, to qualify as a finisher, had to complete the voyage not later than September 11th, 1960.

Each entrant was required to carry, as safety equipment, an inflatable life raft, radar reflector, portable loud-hailer, foghorn, daylight distress signals and marker dye, flares and pyrotechnic distress signals. No physical contact, except for the passing of written messages, could be made with other craft at sea and no stores could be received from any other ship during the race. Yachts were permitted to put in anywhere, and to anchor or moor for any purpose during the race, but when at sea were required to be fully independent and capable of carrying out their own emergency repairs.

Race awards, presented by *The Observer*, comprised a trophy, consisting of a salver depicting a map of the Atlantic, to the first competitor to arrive at the finishing line, a smaller salver of the same design to the second competitor to finish, and replicas of the salver to other competitors finishing within the specified time.

Gipsy Moth III — FRANCIS CHICHESTER

The winner of the race. Time: 40 days. Yawl, designed by Robert Clark and built by John Tyrell at Arklow, Eire, in 1959. Self-steering gear designed by owner and built by Agamemnon Boatyard, Buckler's Hard.

Length, overall	.. 39 ft. 7 in.
Length, waterline	.. 28 ft. 0 in.
Beam (max.)	.. 10 ft. $1\frac{3}{4}$ in.
Draft	.. 6 ft. 5 in.
Thames tonnage	.. 13 tons
Gross tonnage	.. $10\frac{3}{4}$ tons
Iron keel	.. $4\frac{1}{4}$ tons

Sail areas

Mainsail	.. $380\frac{1}{2}$ sq. ft.
Genoa	.. 380 sq. ft.
Trisail	.. 144 sq. ft.
Storm jib	.. 65 sq. ft.

Course: Great Circle course, Plymouth–New York, approx. 3,100 miles (4,004 miles actually covered). Averaged $76\frac{1}{2}$ miles per day, on course towards New York, or almost 100 miles per day actually sailed.*

* Methods of calculating daily runs varied among the competitors. Chichester and Howells appear sometimes to have taken their patent log readings (i.e. distances actually sailed). Hasler recorded the shortest line between successive 0900 hours G.M.T. positions. My own method was to note the distance covered in the direction of the objective between successive noon G.M.T. positions. All distances are in sea miles.

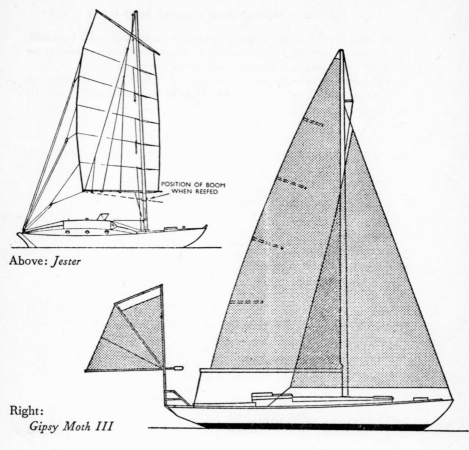

Above: *Jester*

POSITION OF BOOM
WHEN REEFED

Right:
Gipsy Moth III

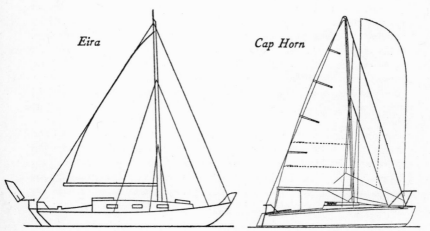

Eira

Cap Horn

On wind, 636 hours (65 per cent. time); Wind free, 288 hours (approx. 30 per cent.); Bare poles, 48 hours; Fog, totalled 336 hours; Calms: says there were not many and they gave him time to sleep.

Sail changes: Reefed main, 16 times; set trisail, 7 times; no main or trisail 24 times; boomed-out jibs, 4 times; major changes headsail, 43 times; Spinnaker not used.

Jester — LT.-COL. H. G. HASLER

Second man home. Time: 48 days. Modified Scandinavian Folkboat with Chinese lug rig on an unstayed mast. Built 1952.

Length, overall	25.9 ft.
Length, waterline	20 ft. 0 in.
Beam	7 ft. 3 in.
Draft	4 ft. 0 in.
Iron keel	1 ton
Displacement (light)	2½ tons
Thames tonnage	5 tons
Single sail area	240 sq. ft.

Course: Followed northern route—higher than Great Circle route—past SW corner of Ireland, curving up to 57° N, 30° W. Distance, 3,417 miles. Averaged 65 miles per day, or 71 miles per day actually sailed. Longest runs, two of 120 miles. No record available of frequent sail adjustments. Return voyage: Sheepshead Bay, Brooklyn to the Needles, I.O.W., 3,417 miles in 38 days 9 hours; average, 86 miles per day.

Cardinal Vertue — DAVID LEWIS

Third man home. Time: 56 days elapsed time (including return after dismasting); 54 days actual time.

Course: Great Circle course (3,100 miles). Average sailed, 57.4 miles per day; able to lay course only 40 per cent. of time, remainder prevented by headwinds or calms. On wind, 758 hours (70 per cent. of time); Wind free, 286 hours (22 per cent. of time); Calms encountered on 37 days (67 per cent. days of voyage) and totalled 183 hours, or 7 days 15 hours, (15 per cent. of time). Fog, 308 hours. Longest run, 102 miles.

Sail changes: Major changes of headsails, 87 times; reefed mainsail, 43 times; lowered mainsail, 3 times; Spinnaker used 10 times for total of 93 hours.

Remarks: Genoa was always left on stay and No. 1 staysail kept set and drawing well when genoa was set, yet time lost in sail changing was considerable. Had to heave-to during reefing, or unreefing the mainsail for 7–15 minutes (86 times) and when reefing staysail (12 times). Estimating the average time stopped at 10 minutes per operation, total time lost was 16½ hours, in contrast to Hasler on *Jester* who made many and exact sail changes virtually without stopping his ship.

RETURN VOYAGE: NEW YORK—ST. JOHN'S—LERWICK, SHETLAND ISLES

New York–St. John's, Newfoundland

Distance: Sailed with Fiona; 1,113 miles covered in 12 days 10 hours 40 minutes. Best day's run: 124 miles; worst, 58 miles. Average, 88 miles per day. On wind, 49 hours; wind free, 260½ hours; able to lay course, 73 per cent. of time. Fog, 16 hours over 4 days; calms, 3 hours over 3 days.

Sail changes: Reefed mainsail 11 times and lowered once because of wind strength; reefed staysail once, major headsail changes, 6 times.

St. John's, Newfoundland–Lerwick, Shetland Isles

Sailed single-handed, September 5th to October 1st, 1960. Distance, 1,984 miles covered in 25 days 21 hours. Average, 77 miles per day. Best day's run, 120 miles; worst, 10 miles. Able to lay course 408 hours (66 per cent. of time); unable to lay course, 213 hours; on wind, 182 hours; off wind, 419 hours. Calms totalled 30 hours including 23½ hours continuous calm after sighting Shetland; fog, 29 hours over 6 days; gales, hove-to 4 times, total of 48½ hours, all during first three weeks.

Sail changes: Reefed main, 12 times. Sailed without main, 15 days 4 hours, three-fifths of time but never in last 5 days. (This was not always through stress of weather; she sailed faster and steered more easily when broad-reaching or running with genoa alone. The mainsail is less than 80 per cent. of the area of the genoa.); Reefed No. 1 staysail, 3 times; changed headsails, 20 times. Ship was steered throughout by wind-vane except in very light airs (when ship's speed fell below 2 knots) and in winds over about 50 m.p.h.

Total time: New York to Lerwick: 38 days 11 hours.

Eira — VAL HOWELLS

Fourth man home. Time: 63 days, elapsed time (including 8 days in Bermuda). Sailing time: 55 days. Folkboat, sloop-rigged.

Length, overall	..	25 ft. 0 in.
Length, waterline	..	19 ft. 6 in.
Beam	..	7 ft. 2 in.
Draft	..	3 ft. 9 in.
Thames tonnage	..	5 tons

Sail areas

Mainsail	..	200 sq. ft.
No. 1 staysail	..	50 sq. ft.
No. 2 staysail	..	30 sq. ft.
Genoa	..	180 sq. ft.
Total sail area	..	380 sq. ft.

Course: Distance sailed by log, 4,125 miles. Average sailed, 75 miles per day. Average made good on direct route Plymouth to New York (3,100 miles), 56.3 miles per day. Longest run, 129 miles.

Head winds, 58 per cent. of time, mostly early in voyage. Wind free, 35 per cent. of time. Calms, 117 hours (7 per cent. of time) including one continuous calm of 31 hours. Fog, about 12 hours. Self-steering not effective in very light winds; also overcome by big quartering swells.

Sail changes: Major headsail changes, 56 times; reefed mainsail, 11 times; handed mainsail, 21 times, mostly in calms or when running under genoa.

Cap Horn — JEAN LACOMBE

Fifth man home. Time: 74 days, elapsed time (started 5 days late); 69 days sailing time. Sloop; plywood construction with centreboard and 400 kg. ballast keel. Designed by J. J. Herbulot. Self-steering gear designed by M. Giannoli.

Length, overall	..	6·5 m. (21·3 ft.)
Length, waterline	..	6·0 m. (19·7 ft.)
Beam (max.)	..	2·27 m. (7·5 ft.)
Beam (waterline)	..	1·9 m. (6·2 ft.)
Draft (centreboard up)	..	0·6 m. (2 ft.)
Displacement (light)	..	900 kg. (1,980 lb.)
Displacement (loaded)	..	3 tonnes (2·95 tons)

Sail areas

Mainsail	..	12·5 sq. m. (134½ sq. ft.)
No. 1 staysail	..	9·3 sq. m. (100 sq. ft.)
No. 2 staysail	..	5·9 sq. m. (68½ sq. ft.)
Genoa	..	12·6 sq. m. (135 sq. ft.)
Tourmentin	..	2·0 sq. m. (21½ sq. ft.)

Course: Average sailed, 61 miles per day; average made good on direct route Plymouth to New York (3,100 miles), 45 miles per day. The craft was so light and its motion so violent that Lacombe was unable to sleep properly.

In his first two weeks out from Plymouth Jean Lacombe covered 450 and 500 miles respectively. During the third week he passed between the Azores, resisting a strong temptation to call there and fix the self-steering gear which was giving trouble, and by July 13th he was half-way across. At this rate of progress he would have equalled or bettered my time. On July 25th he ran into a severe gale and lay to a sea-anchor, first from the bow, and then from the stern where it proved more effective, even though he was swept by a wave which lifted the hatch and swamped the cabin. Calms followed the gales so that by July 29th he had covered only 250 miles in 13 days. To avoid the August hurricanes he altered course to the north, a most seamanlike decision in my opinion, though it meant being headed by the Gulf Stream.

By August 18th he was off the Nantucket Shoals lightship where he was taken in tow by a Coastguard cutter as he was in the path of hurricane "Cleo". When "Cleo" changed course a few hours later he cast off the tow and reached the Ambrose light on August 24th.

I am indebted for this summary of *Cap Horn's* voyage to Jean Lacombe's account in *Le Bateau* and to John Pfleiger, for the translation.

APPENDIX FOUR

Research Observations

The idea of doing some research during the voyage first came to me as a possible excuse for such a long absence. But before long the prospect of breaking fresh ground in a field that had long interested me became an exciting prospect in its own right.

As a basis for research Dr. H. E. Lewis of the Medical Research Council and I prepared the daily "Medical Log" reproduced below, copies of which were given to each of the competitors with the following introduction:

The Single-handed Race is a unique opportunity to learn about the eating habits, the mental and the physical feelings of men in isolation. This sort of information, though very valuable, is usually almost impossible to obtain. In turn it will help us in problems of survival at sea, especially water requirements.

We have listed a number of "feelings" in the log and would like you to tick off the column that is nearest to your mood. Each feeling is matched by its opposite, so from one end of the line to the other there is a broad span of mood. If you think that the words at the end don't apply, or apply equally, tick the middle section.

Bearing in mind that you will have to attend to many other things, we have tried to keep this daily log down to a minimum. We greatly appreciate the trouble you are taking. Be assured that any personal information will be treated privately and confidentially.   DAVID LEWIS

In collaboration with H. E. LEWIS,
Medical Research Council, London, N.W.3

Many months will still be needed to analyse the mass of data we obtained from these daily Medical Logs, and the following are merely some tentative ideas which the work suggests at the present stage.

Eating and sleeping habits: We studied these because man, being a social animal, is conditioned in his activities by sociological conventions and it is, therefore, very difficult to discover his natural biological patterns of behaviour. Are there inherent sleep rhythms? How much sleep do we really need? Are our meal times dictated by physical necessity or by custom and convenience? These are some of the questions whose answers we do not yet know.

There are two situations where human beings are practically isolated from

1 JULY 1960

A. *How do you feel?*

	Applies very strongly	Applies	Both apply or neither apply	Applies	Applies very strongly	
My normal self						Seeing things
Exhausted						Fresh
Lonely						Completely self-sufficient
Enjoy cooking						Can't be bothered about food
Poor appetite						Hungry
Calm						Irritable
Feelings have been constant						Feelings have changed a lot during the day
Tense and excited						Calm and relaxed
Confident						Scared
Keen to do well						Uncertain, sorry I started
Bored						Not bored: too much to do
My normal self						Hearing things
A new confident mood						Wish it were all over
Sexy						Not sexy
Happy without feminine company						Would enjoy company of other sex

Other moods:

B. *Water:* What did you use today?

Fresh water: ....Drinking (including beverages)
...............Cooking
...............Washing and waste
Sea Water: ....Cooking

C. *Food:* What did you eat today? | Times
Underline what you heated and cooked.

the pressure of social convention; in Polar expeditions, and when alone at sea. Polar parties are, of course, groups, so they must conform to a minimum of social organization. On the other hand, they live in conditions of continuous daylight or continuous darkness, so a sense of clock time does not dominate their routine, and they will tend to organize their meal times, and their "day and night", in accordance with convenience and their biological requirements.

In single-handed sailing, extraneous social connections are completely

1 JULY 1960

D. *Physical feeling*

Do you feel absolutely A.1 ?

If not, what do you feel is wrong, how severe,
and which part of your body ?

E. *Sleep, naps and interruptions*

24 Hours (State whether G.M.T. or Ship's Time)

From Yesterday | 1 2 3 4 5 6 7 8 9 10 11 12 13 14 15 16 17 18 19 20 21 22 23 24 | Contd. Tomorrow

Cause of interruptions :

Did you dream ?

F. *General comments* (to give full picture)

G. *What time did you fill up this form ?*

...............hrs.

absent. Food and sleep are taken according to need, modified by the availability of artificial light and fuel, the stresses of weather and working ship, proximity to land, shipping lanes, ice, etc.

Sleep: The experience of four recent Polar expeditions has been that, in spite of great disruptions in sleep, the average is almost exactly eight hours. This figure does not vary significantly whether or not "cat naps" are taken;

nor is it effected by exercise; nor does it differ between the Polar night and day.*

Racing to windward alone in a small yacht, sleep is often broken and at times sadly lacking. I, personally, found my judgment to be so seriously impaired during periods of lack of sleep that I made serious errors, in spite of being on my guard. Two examples were, closing the cliffs of Nova Scotia, and running aground off Vineyard Sound. Our average hours of sleep were 6·7 hours per night. Quality of sleep is as important as its length and undoubtedly varies. But how to measure and study "depth" of sleep is a difficult problem.

Food: Hasler lost nineteen pounds during the race. I also lost nineteen pounds, in spite of heavier physical work, and some food and water shortages. I lost no weight on the return trip.

Our eating patterns varied. Mine, during the race, showed long periods without food, followed by close-spaced groups of meals. This tendency is also present in the records of Hasler and Howells, and of my trip back; but it is less obvious and tends to be masked by "nibbling". Nevertheless, the eating pattern seems to have been dictated more by biological needs and the demands of sailing than by conventional meal times.

Studies of mood: A few tentative conclusions are now emerging.

(i) Solitude is not at all the same as loneliness, e.g. the loneliness that a friendless person experiences in a big city. We were rarely lonely on our voyages. Even during the long, awe-inspiring nights, illumined by the Northern Lights of the homeward journey, I did not feel lonely.

(ii) Observations noted *at the time* are the only valid ones. Memory very quickly plays tricks; usually seeing our behaviour and emotions in a better light than they really deserved. For instance, I honestly forgot that I had been frightened at all during one gale, until I looked up my notes.

(iii) The degree of fear varied with the individual; one (not me), did not suffer acute fear at all. In general there are two types of fear: (*a*) initial tension and anxiety, lasting for the first few days at sea, and then replaced by calm confidence and enjoyment; (*b*) after this we were only afraid with due reason, as in gales.

(iv) A relaxed confidence, a sense of being "at one" with the ocean and its winds, was our main emotional state, after the period of adjustment had passed. This state was often temporarily disrupted by such events as calms, shortages of books or exhausting sail-changing but tended to become re-established when conditions allowed.

(v) Hallucinations seem to occur only when solitude and fatigue are

* *Sleep Patterns on Polar Expeditions.* By Dr. H. E. Lewis. Ciba Foundation Symposium on "Nature of Sleep", 1961.

accompanied by monotonous occupations. Thus, long hours of continuous steering sometimes caused them, but because of the efficient operation of our wind-vanes, they were minimal. This observation may have some bearing on space flight. Possibly the rhythmic effect of monotonous activities tends to induce auto-hypnosis. Whatever the mechanism, I would think that varying tasks demanding physical and or mental effort could be valuable in preserving emotional stability.

Acknowledgments

Grateful acknowledgment is due to the following who have taken part, or are still participating in the work involved in this research project:

Dr. H. E. Lewis, Division of Human Physiology, National Institute of Medical Research.

Dr. D. Hollingsworth, Dr. Neil Beaton, Dr. E. C. Drescher, of New York, Dr. J. C. Lilly of the U.S. Virgin Isles, Dr. W. H. Sebrell, Jnr. and Professor E. L. Severinghouse, M.D., both of Columbia University, and Mr. J. M. Harries, Ministry of Agriculture and Fisheries.

APPENDIX FIVE

Treatment of Sea-serpent Stings and Other Ailments

The following is virtually a reprint of the "Medical Advice to Competitors" notes which were compiled and circulated before the race, together with medical kits and emergency stores supplied through the generosity of the manufacturers.

I feel that the general principles and approach to the question of illness, accident and survival, when alone or short-handed and far from help, are valid. A part of this approach, however, was the full use of modern antibiotics and other powerful remedies; the very progress of medicine soon renders particular products out-dated. The named drugs and dressings, therefore, should be treated as examples only.

For this appendix to be of any use, it should be regarded only as a frame-work, whose interstices may be readily filled in with the aid of some of those innumerable medical men who have become hopelessly infected by love of the sea or the waste places of the earth.

During about two hundred and ninety man-days of solo sailing, apart from initial seasickness, sundry cuts and bruises, and my bump on the head, competitors in the race were fortunate in keeping fit and well throughout their passages.

Medical Advice to Competitors

HEALTH, MEDICAL EQUIPMENT AND EMERGENCY SURVIVAL

by David H. Lewis, M.B., Ch.B.

AIM OF MEDICAL ADVICE

People quickly go to pieces when morale breaks down; it is best maintained by knowing what to do.

Stop short of exhaustion, keep something in reserve; lack of rest warps judgment and impairs efficiency.

Eat and drink what suits you best; sweet foods and drinks are useful when very tired. The only vitamin you need is Vitamin C (anti-scurvy).

Keep the skin clean; severe boils and painful and disabling infections of the skin are caused by ingrained dirt and crusted salt. Fresh water is well spared for washing at times. Bare feet (when practicable) help prevent "Athlete's Foot" (infection between the toes).

A protective cream against sun and salt is provided.

MEDICAL EQUIPMENT

Only a few remedies can be carried, so selection has had to be arbitrary and advice dogmatic. In general, minor ills, accidents and symptoms can best be left to nature and common sense. Some of the drugs here are powerful, so you should show the list to your own doctor to check for individual sensitivity, or to add anything you personally may need.

NOTE

Alcohol. This is a matter of personal taste; it has no medical value.

Stimulants, sedatives and "tranquillizers" vary in their effects with different people and according to circumstances. None is included. If you wish to take any, you are strongly advised to consult your own doctor.

GUIDE TO TREATMENT

Wounds and bleeding. Wash off dirt. Apply an Elastoplast dressing or apply antiseptic cream (No. 10), then a standard dressing (No. 13), or Elastoplast. *Firm* bandaging of a pad over a wound will stop *any* bleeding. Do *not* make a tourniquet, as it will usually increase bleeding by compressing veins but not arteries. If it is applied properly it will cause gangrene, by cutting off the circulation. To close a gaping wound, use interlocking strips of Elastoplast from each side.

In severe wounds, fractures or burns, take the *antibiotic capsules* (No. 1) in a dose of one capsule four times a day for four days (or longer if infection occurs). Take *pain tablets* (No. 3) up to eight a day, or if pain is very severe, take *severe pain tablets* (No. 4) one every four hours, dissolved under the tongue.

Fractures. Antibiotic capsules, if the fracture is associated with wounds (*see above*), and pain tablets (*see above*).

Arm. Strap it to your body with Elastoplast. If you splint the limb, you will automatically use it when you lose your balance, and cause further damage.

Ribs. Leave them alone. No treatment. Do not put Elastoplast round your chest as this will only restrict your breathing and do no good.

Leg. Improvise long splints from floorboards, etc., well padded with clothes, to immobilize joints above and below injury.

Burns. Wash clean, apply antiseptic cream (No. 10) and cover with an Elastoplast dressing if small, or with a standard dressing (No. 13) and crêpe bandage if larger. Do not disturb for several days if comfortable. For large burns also take antibiotic capsules (No. 1) and pain tablets (Nos. 3 or 4) as described under "Wounds".

"Athlete's Foot". Painful cracks between toes. Bare feet. Use powder (No. 11).

Pneumonia, bronchitis, infections of the skin and tissues, fractures, burns and large wounds. Use antibiotic capsules (No. 1) one four times a day for four days, and continue if necessary.

Acute appendicitis (and related conditions). There is severe persistent abdominal pain, repeated vomiting and great tenderness, probably constipation. Prop yourself up in your bunk, take fluids only, and take the antibiotic capsules (No. 1) as above.

Severe diarrhoea. Especially if slime and blood is present. Take the sulphonamide tablets (No. 1) three tablets four times daily, for four to six days.

Preventing scurvy. Take one Vitamin C tablet (No. 5) each day.

MEDICAL SUPPLIES LIST

No. 1. Broad-spectrum antibiotic capsules (Terramycin (S.F.) Caps. Pfizer 100 supplied).

No. 2. Sulphonamide tablets (Succinylsulphathiazole tabs. $\frac{1}{2}$ Gm. 50 supplied).

No. 3. Ordinary pain tablets (Soluble salicylate) (Zactirin tabs. (Wyeth) 300 supplied).

No. 4. Severe pain tablets (Aminode hydrochloride. 5 mg. 25 supplied on individual prescription).

Note. Morphia may so impair judgment that, for a lone sailor who has to rely on himself, it is rather a means towards suicide than a treatment. It has been omitted.

No. 5. Anti-scurvy tablets. Vitamin C. (Ascorbic acid, 50 mg. 50 supplied).

No. 6. Eye-drops to relieve pain to allow removal of foreign bodies. (5 per cent. cocaine drops, 2 drachms. on individual prescription).

No. 7. Eye ointment for inflammation of the eye (1 tube antibiotic and hydrocort. ointment).

Note. Sore red eyes due to stinging of salt spray should be bathed with water only. Use neither the eye drops nor ointment.

No. 8. Protective skin cream against sun and salt. (Prepared by Dr. Hughes of Scientific Pharmaceuticals Ltd.).

No. 9. Waterproof Elastoplast dressings. Three Elastoplast 3-in. bandages. 2 lb. cotton wool. Gauze. 6 crêpe bandages.

No. 10. Antiseptic cream. (Preferably an antibiotic cream.)

No. 11. Powder for Athlete's Foot (Amoxal). (Smith and Nephew) 2 oz.

No. 12. WESCO First Aid Kit containing standard dressings, 1 pair scissors, antiseptic burn and wound creams. Codeine Co. tablets (for pain).

IF FORCED TO ABANDON SHIP

Cold, aggravated by wetness and wind, is the greatest cause of loss of life among castaways (*MacDonald Critchley, 1943*). Therefore, a covered life-raft, in which a "fug" can be produced and heat-loss prevented, is most desirable.

A man can live fifty days without food but usually under two weeks without water. He should not drink salt water, because more fluid is lost from the body through the kidneys in getting rid of the excess salt.

WATER

Carry two gallons in a plastic jerry-can attached to the rubber raft. (This will float, as fresh water is lighter than salt.)

Ration: *None on first day.* Minimum of $1\frac{1}{2}$ pints (900 c.c.) per day. However, $\frac{4}{5}$ pint (500 c.c.) per day will maintain fluid balance for a time, but you will deteriorate gradually.

EMERGENCY FOOD

Protein and fats are harmful with restricted water. Food should be carbohydrate (sweet food) only. Rations: three to four ounces per day (90 gr.) made up of rum fudge, glucose sweets, glucose lemon in the drinking water, Horlick's tablets, etc.

A solar still is provided for use with your life raft.

RARER CONDITIONS

Such accidents as Polar bear bites or sea-serpent stings are certainly uncommon, but are of such great literary interest that they may safely be left to the imagination and initiative of the competitors.

Acknowledgments

Invaluable advice in the preparation of this document was freely given by many people. Sometimes circumstances prevented it being taken in full and the responsibility for final choice and decisions and any consequences thereof, remain my own. Similarly, while this document could not have been prepared without their help, it does not necessarily represent their views.

I wish to thank especially: Surg. Capt. Baskerville, R.N.; Mr. E. C. B. Lee, Secretary, Naval Life Saving Committee; Mr. F. E. Smith, Assistant Secretary, R.N.F.R.C.; Mr. H. Proctor, F.R.C.S., of Birmingham Accident Hospital; Sir Heneage Ogilvie; Dr. H. L'Etang; Prof. Guide Guida; and Mr. A. B. E. de Jong.

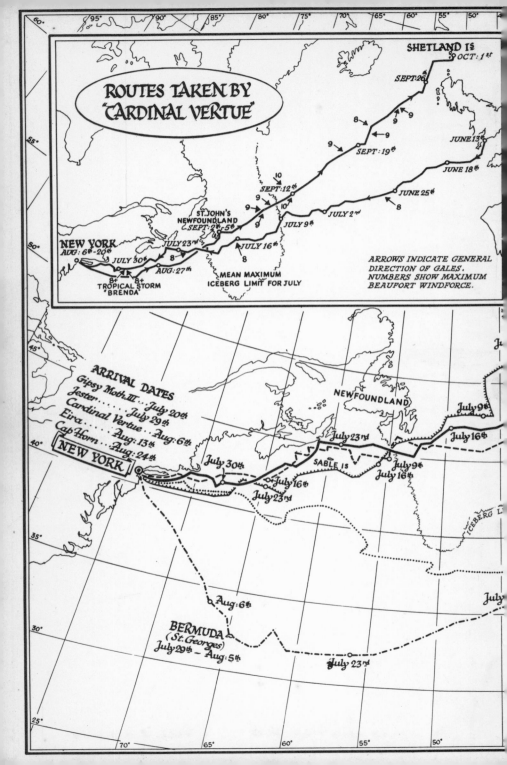

ROUTES TAKEN BY "CARDINAL VERTUE"

SHETLAND IS
OCT: 1st
SEPT: 26th
SEPT: 19th
JUNE 13th
JUNE 18th
JUNE 25th

8
9
9
9
8
9
10
9
10
9
8

SEPT: 12th
ST. JOHN'S
NEWFOUNDLAND
SEPT: 2nd-5th
JULY 2nd
JULY 9th
JULY 16th
JULY 23rd

NEW YORK
AUG: 6th-20th
JULY 30th
8
AUG: 27th
8
8+
8+
TROPICAL STORM
"BRENDA"

MEAN MAXIMUM
ICEBERG LIMIT FOR JULY

ARROWS INDICATE GENERAL
DIRECTION OF GALES.
NUMBERS SHOW MAXIMUM
BEAUFORT WINDFORCE.

ARRIVAL DATES
Gipsy Moth III .. July 20th
Jester . . . . . July 29th
Cardinal Vertue . . Aug: 6th
Eira . . . . . Aug: 13th
Cap Horn . . Aug: 24th

NEW YORK

NEWFOUNDLAND

July 9th
July 16th
July 23rd
SABLE IS
July 9th
July 16th

July 30th
July 16th
July 23rd

ICEBERG L

July

Aug: 6th

BERMUDA
(St. Georges)
July 29th - Aug: 5th

July 23rd